Frederick Walter Lowndes

The Extension of the Contagious Diseases acts to Liverpool

and other Seaports

practically considered

Frederick Walter Lowndes

The Extension of the Contagious Diseases acts to Liverpool and other Seaports
practically considered

ISBN/EAN: 9783337815806

Printed in Europe, USA, Canada, Australia, Japan

Cover: Foto ©Andreas Hilbeck / pixelio.de

More available books at **www.hansebooks.com**

THE EXTENSION

OF THE

CONTAGIOUS DISEASES ACTS

TO

LIVERPOOL

AND OTHER SEAPORTS

PRACTICALLY CONSIDERED.

BY

FREDERICK W. LOWNDES, M. R. C. S., ENG.,

SURGEON TO THE LIVERPOOL LOCK HOSPITAL,
LOCAL HONORARY SECRETARY TO THE ASSOCIATION FOR PROMOTING THE
EXTENSION OF THE CONTAGIOUS DISEASES ACTS.

LIVERPOOL: ADAM HOLDEN, 48, CHURCH STREET.
LONDON: J. & A. CHURCHILL, NEW BURLINGTON STREET.
GLASGOW: JAMES MACLEHOSE.
BRISTOL: J. E. CHILLCOTT.
SHEFFIELD.: THOMAS RODGERS.

1876.

CONTENTS.

INTRODUCTION.

"THERE are few questions less inviting, though there are few more important in reference to public health, than those which refer to the extent and the character of venereal disease as it comes under observation in great towns. Are these maladies on the increase? Are they undergoing any modification in their type? These are queries the answers to which would have no little value in relation to social as well as to medical science."

Such is the commencing paragraph of a Paper contributed in the *Medical Times and Gazette*, of the 28th September, 1861, by the Liverpool correspondent of that journal, who proceeds to give a most interesting account of the various local institutions in which patients suffering from venereal diseases are received, and concludes as follows : "It is, I think, only fair to infer that there has been in this town a perceptible diminution in the amount of disease among the lowest class of prostitutes, and a decided mitigation in the type of the disease itself. At the dispensary attached to the Lying-in-Hospital, as well as at the other dispensaries, a good deal of infantile syphilis is found, and I have no evidence to prove any diminution of these patients."

The above questions, though no more inviting, are cer-

tainly no less important at the present than they were at that
time, now nearly fifteen years ago. Since then the subject
has received much more attention at the hands of the medical
profession in general, as many diseases of the internal organs,
the liver, brain, lungs, etc., etc., and various affections of
the eye, which were all formerly supposed to depend on other
causes, are now recognised as of syphilitic origin. Few
meetings occur at medical societies at which some pathological specimen of syphilitic disease is not exhibited, or some
case of a similar character involving features of interest, is
not detailed. The whole subject of the pathology of syphilis
has recently been brought before the Pathological Society of
London, by Mr. Jonathan Hutchinson, and the discussion
which followed, occupying several entire meetings, was one
of the most interesting and exhaustive which has ever taken
place.

HISTORY OF THE CONTAGIOUS DISEASES ACTS.

THE frightful prevalence and virulence of disease among the lower class of prostitutes in certain seaports, garrison towns, and in the neighbourhood of camps, had for many years attracted the serious attention of the legislature, and in the year following the publication of the Paper referred to in our Introduction, a special committee was appointed by the Government to inquire into the prevalence of venereal disease in the army and navy. Their report, dated December 15th, 1862, contains, at its conclusion, the following :—

" Your committee have refrained from entering into the painful details which have come to their knowledge of the state of our naval and military stations at home as regards prostitution. These facts are so appalling that they feel it a duty to press on the Government the necessity of at once grappling with the mass of vice, filth, and disease which surrounds the soldiers' barracks and the seamen's homes, which not only crowds our hospitals with sick, weakens the roll of our effectives, and swells the lists of our invalids, but which surely, however slowly, saps the vigour of our soldiers and our seamen, sows the seeds of degradation and degeneracy, and causes an amount of suffering difficult to overestimate."

The reports of Government committees are not, as a rule, of a sensational description, much more generally they are somewhat dry and technical documents. The statements of witnesses are, after repeated cross-examination and re-examination, stripped of all sensational details, and more attention is paid to facts than mere opinions. Very terrible, then, must have been the state of matters when a Government Committee concluded their report in such terms as these. It resulted, about two years subsequently, in the passing of "An Act for the Prevention of Contagious Diseases at certain Naval and Military Stations, 1864." This, though experimental and in many respects imperfect, was the means of effecting an immense amount of benefit to the lower class of prostitutes, as well as a considerable diminution of disease in the localities where it was enforced, in Portsmouth, Plymouth, and Devonport.

In this same year (1864) a committee, consisting of the most eminent physicians and surgeons in London, was appointed by the Admiralty to inquire into the pathology and treatment of syphilis, and to suggest practical rules for the prevention of venereal diseases, capable of being adopted by the naval and military authorities. The inquiry lasted over a period of nearly two years, and among the sixty witnesses examined were Sir William Jenner, Sir James Paget, Sir William Fergusson, Dr. Robert Barnes, the late Mr. Acton, Mr. Bowman, Mr. Erichsen, Professor Boeck, of Christiania, Dr. Arthur Farre, Mr. Hilton, the late Professor Syme, Mr. Erasmus Wilson, Mr. Prescott Hewett, the late Sir William Lawrence, Mr. James R. Lane, several medical officers of the army and navy, and other witnesses. The result of this inquiry was, that a mass of facts and practical experience was accumulated, in reference to the pathology and treatment of syphilis, such as had rarely or never been before collected to elucidate the nature of any one disease ; and the report of the commissioners is one of the most valuable medical works we possess. The attention of the commissioners had been especially drawn to the laws which had been enforced in Malta, in which island the regular periodical examination of all known prostitutes, and the detention in hospital of any who were found diseased, had resulted in the extinction of venereal disease, so far as the island was concerned, all fresh cases being traced to importation. The Act of 1866 was framed according to the recommendations of the commission, and contained provisions somewhat similar to those in force at Malta, but with many important additions. Thus, Clause 12 provides that " A hospital shall not be certified under this Act, unless at the time of the granting of a certificate adequate provision is made for the moral and religious instruction of the women detained therein under this Act; and if at any subsequent time it appears to the Admiralty, or the Secretary of State for War, that in any such hospital adequate provision for that purpose is not made, the certificate for that hospital shall be withdrawn." Moreover, Clause 27 provides that " Every woman shall, on her discharge from the hospital, be sent to the place of her residence, if she so desires, without expense to herself."

This Act, which is entitled " An Act for the better Prevention of Contagious Diseases at certain Naval and Military Stations," repealed the Act of 1864, and with some alterations, to be presently noticed, is the Act now in force. Its benefits were so great, physically, morally, and socially, in the localities where it was extended, that an association was formed in London for its extension to the civil population. Its associates comprised the most eminent members of the medical profession, many clergymen of high position, the leading educational authorities at the universities, and many other persons eminent as statesmen and philanthropists. Public meetings were held, and influential petitions for the extension of the Acts were presented to Parliament.

In consequence of these, a Committee of the House of

Lords was, in 1868, appointed to consider the subject, and their report contains the following recommendation :—

"The committee consider that the cautious extension of the Act may be safely entrusted to the Government, and therefore recommend the introduction into Parliament, at the earliest practicable opportunity, of a Bill giving to Her Majesty in Council power to apply the Act of 1866, first, to all naval and military stations ; and, secondly, to any locality the inhabitants of which may apply to be included in the operations of the Act, and be able to submit satisfactory proof upon the following points, viz., that adequate hospital accommodation can be provided and maintained ; that the necessary arrangements can be made for the religious and moral care of the inmates of such hospital or ward, according to the provisions of the Act, and that the police force is efficient."

The witnesses examined before this committee comprised, among others, Sir William Jenner, Mr. Prescott Hewett, the late Mr. Acton, Mr. Berkeley Hill, Sir James Paget, the late Mr. Skey, and Dr. Trench, the Medical Officer of Health for Liverpool.

In 1869 a Committee of the House of Commons was appointed "To inquire into the working of the Contagious Diseases Act, 1866, and to consider whether, and how far, and under what conditions, it may be expedient to extend its operations." Being nearly at the end of the session, the committee confined their inquiries to those districts in which the Act had been applied, and to the alterations thought necessary to secure more satisfactory results. Their report commences as follows :—

"Although the Act has only been in operation two years and a half, and at some stations only seven months, strong testimony is borne to the benefits, both in a moral and sanitary point of view, which have already resulted from it.

"Prostitution appears to have diminished, its worst

features to have been softened, and its physical evils abated."

This committee recommended certain alterations in the Act of 1866, among which were these :—

(1.) That the limits should be extended to 15 miles at the present districts, instead of 5.

(4.) That the certificate of discharge from hospital should be given to the police, and not to the women.

(5.) That the visiting surgeon should have power to authorise any woman to discontinue her attendance for examination, on his ascertaining, through the inspector of police, that she had abandoned a life of prostitution.

(7.) That the following places should be included in the schedule of the Act :—Gravesend, Maidstone, Winchester, Dover, Deal and Walmer, Canterbury, Dartmouth, Ivy Bridge, and Southampton.

Their report concludes as follows :—

" Your committee would remark, in conclusion, that whilst, for the reasons stated at the commencement of their report, they have confined their investigations to the object of securing greater efficiency in the treatment of these diseases at military and naval stations, they recommend that further inquiry, by a committee appointed early in the next session, should be instituted, with the view of ascertaining whether it would be practicable to extend to the civil population the benefits of an Act which has already done so much to diminish prostitution, decrease disease, and reclaim the abandoned."

The Acts of 1864 and 1866 both passed with very little opposition ; but after the formation of the association for promoting the extension of the Acts, and the report of the committee of the House of Lords, a very strong opposition arose; and when the recommendations of the committee of the House of Commons had been adopted in the Act of 1869, which passed on the 11th August, in that year, this opposition gathered considerable strength. In 1870, the first motion for the repeal of the Acts was brought before the House of Commons, the debate being held with closed doors. The motion was negatived by a large majority, and a promise was made by the Government that a Royal Commission should be appointed to consider the question in all its bearings.

I have given these various details as completely, and yet concisely, as I could, in order that a clear insight may be obtained as to why these Acts were ever passed, and, having been passed, why they were continued and extended. It will be seen that the first Act was passed after a committee of the Government had pressed upon it the necessity of at once grappling with the mass of vice, filth, and disease which surrounded the soldiers' barracks and the seamen's homes. Hence the assertion that this Act was hastily passed, and without due consideration, is entirely disproved, since the Act of 1864 was not passed till nearly two years after the report of the committee had been sent in.

Again, the object of the Act was the prevention of disease, the preamble being as follows :—

"Whereas, it is expedient to make provisions calculated to prevent the spreading of certain contagious diseases in the places to which this Act applies. Be it therefore enacted," etc.

And here we see how utterly groundless is the assertion so repeatedly and recklessly made, that these Acts were passed to make vice easy and sin safe.

The Act of 1866 was passed in accordance with the recommendations of the highest medical authorities, after a most laborious and painstaking inquiry, extending over a period of two years; and special committees of both the House of Lords and the House of Commons recommended its extension, which was partly adopted in the Act of 1869. The idea of repealing these Acts does not appear to have been even entertained by any member of these committees; and it was not till 1870, six years after the first Act had been passed, that the motion for repeal was brought forward, and the Royal Commission appointed.

Before passing on to their report, it is of great importance that we should know which are the various localities in which the Acts are in force. The following is a complete list, copied from the first schedule of the Act of 1869 :—

PLACES WHERE THE CONTAGIOUS DISEASES ACTS ARE
ENFORCED.

In England.

Aldershot.	Portsmouth.
Canterbury.	Sheerness.
Chatham.	Shorncliffe (including
Colchester.	Walmer, Deal, and
Dover.	Folkestone).
Gravesend.	Southampton.
Maidstone.	Winchester.
Plymouth and Devonport	Windsor.
(including Dartmouth).	Woolwich.

In Ireland.

The Curragh.	Cork.	Queenstown.

From this it will be seen that the Acts are at present

applied only to some garrison towns and certain naval seaports; the large seaports of Liverpool, Bristol, Hull, Cardiff, etc., being very conspicuous by their absence. It is most important that this list should be carefully studied and frequently referred to, as it is surprising how much ignorance there is, even amongst people whom we should expect to find well-informed on the subject. It will help us to understand how, on the one hand, these Acts are too partially applied to have any influence in reducing disease beyond the very limited respective areas to which they are applied. On the other hand, the districts are sufficiently numerous and variable to enable us to judge of the effects produced by the Acts in a medical, moral, and social aspect, in large and small towns; and to afford everyone who may wish to be better informed an opportunity of making inquiries from friends resident in these districts, or, what is far better, by personal observations on the spot.

The Royal Commissioners, as at first appointed, were twenty-five in number; but two, Lieutenant-General Peel and Mr. George Campbell, were only able to attend some of the earlier meetings, and their names are not appended to the report. As showing the thoroughly representative character of the Commission, I give here their names:—

The Right Honourable William Nathaniel Massey, Chairman; the Right Honourable Viscount Hardinge; the Right Reverend the Bishop of Carlisle; the Right Honourable Lord Hampton; the Right Honourable W. F. Cowper-Temple; Sir J. Salusbury Trelawny, Bart.; Sir Walter C. James, Bart.; Vice-Admiral Collinson; Charles Buxton, Esq.; Major O'Reilly, M.P.; Peter Rylands, Esq., M.P.; A. J. Mundella, Esq., M.P.; Professor Huxley; the Rev. Canon Gregory; the late Rev. J. F. D. Maurice; the Rev. Dr. Hannah; Dr. Samuel Wilks; Dr. J. H. Bridges; Dr. G. E. Paget; Timothy Holmes, Esq., F.R.C.S.; the late

Holmes Coote, Esq.; G. W. Hastings, Esq.; Mr. Robert Applegarth.

It will be seen that the clergy, the bar, the medical profession, the army and navy, were all well represented on the commission, which, as will appear, comprised both supporters and opponents of the Acts, while a large proportion may be fairly regarded as neutral. The commissioners commenced to take evidence on the 11th December, 1870. Eighty witnesses were examined, amongst whom were various official personages and officers of high rank in the public services:—Mr. Vernon Lushington, Secretary of the Admiralty; Captain Harris, Assistant Commissioner of Metropolitan Police, and five superior officers of the force; the Inspector of Certified Hospitals, and nine surgeons engaged in the administration of the Acts; various persons officially connected with different lock hospitals, refuges, and reformatories; besides many others—magistrates, clergymen of the Established Church, and of different denominations.

It is impossible to give briefly a fair *resumé* of the commissioners' report, as their recommendations were not absolutely favourable, either to the opponents or supporters of the Acts; and the report has appended to it no fewer than seven different dissents, to all of which it is only fair, as well as courteous, to give due consideration. The report, which is signed by all the commissioners, gives a summary of the evidence taken before them, which confirms most completely the conclusions arrived at by the special committees of the House of Lords and House of Commons respectively; and, as the commissioners had been empowered to suggest whether the Acts should be amended, maintained, extended, or repealed, we find many other subjects treated in the report to which the select committees did not allude, their duties having been confined to the question of extension only. Representatives of the two societies which were formed for the purposes respectively of extending and repealing the Acts were permitted to be present at the meetings of the commissioners, to watch the proceedings, and suggest witnesses to be examined. The alleged abuses of power by the police, which had been made the subject of sensational speeches at public meetings, first claims attention ; and nothing can be stronger than the language of the commissioners on this point. I give the whole of the paragraph (23) which relates to this :—

"Among the means adopted by some of the opponents of the Acts, to bring them into public odium, have been charges of misconduct or gross negligence on the part of the police in putting the law in force against common prostitutes. Cases have been brought forward in publications and speeches at public meetings, not only of cruel insults offered to innocent women through the agency of the Acts, but of repeated wrongs to the unhappy women who have been or are subjected to them. We have made inquiries into every case in which names and details were given. We have requested the persons who have publicly made these statements to substantiate them. In some instances, the persons thus challenged have refused to come forward ; in others, the explanation has been hearsay, or more or less frivolous. The result of our inquiries has been to satisfy us that the police are not chargeable with any abuse of their authority, and that they have hitherto discharged a novel and difficult duty with moderation and caution. Even if it had been proved that they had in some instances made mistakes, or exceeded their duty, such errors might have rendered it necessary to make provision for the more careful administration of the Acts, but would have been no valid argument for their repeal. The charges thus rashly made and repeated have contributed much to excite public indignation against these enactments."

A large amount of evidence was received on the subject of venereal disease; its classification, and the character of its different forms; its diagnostics; its effects on the constitution of the sufferers (whether by their own fault, or, as in some cases, by innocent contact), and of the conditions under which it becomes more or less contagious, and susceptible of treatment. After citing various medical authorities, as to the prevalence and severity of the disease, as to which there are differences of opinion, the commissioners remark (par 26) :—

" Substantially, however, the authorities are agreed that the disease is contagious; that, even in the milder form of gonorrhœa, 'it sometimes involves for a time painful, and even disabling complications, and cannot absolutely be said never to leave permanent local damage behind it'; that many innocent persons, married and unmarried, including medical men and nurses, may, and do, suffer from the contagion, and that the posterity of a diseased parent are liable to serious affection from constitutional syphilis."

The various statistics brought before the commissioners in the returns of the army and navy medical departments; the metropolitan police returns, showing the number of brothels and public women, and of the proportions of disease in the protected districts, at various periods since the Act of 1864, received great attention from them.

In paragraph 36, they say :—

" The statistical tables above examined were put in to prove the effect upon the health of the army and navy of the new system. The police returns, put in by Captain Harris, the Assistant Commissioner of Metropolitan Police, and explained by him, show that, in 1866, before periodical examinations had been introduced, and when the Act of 1864

only was in force, *out of an aggregate number of* 1,661
examinations made, 1,103 *were of women found to be
diseased.*"

Again, in paragraph 38, they say :—

"But though the numerical results of the statistics
referred to must be, for the reasons above stated, incon-
clusive, we think it right to observe that, so far as the army
and navy are concerned, the evidence before us appears
to testify to a general impression on the part of the medical
officers of both services, that the Acts have operated bene-
ficially on the health of the man. A striking proof of this
is contained in the evidence of Dr. Balfour, who has been
induced by further experience to change his view entirely as
to the probable success of the present Acts in repressing the
disease against which they were chiefly directed, viz., constitutional syphilis. Dr. Balfour, who dissented strongly from
the recommendations of the Medical Committee of 1864,
especially with reference to periodical examinations, now
testifies that the working of the Acts has been 'decidedly
beneficial,' and that the periodical examination of women
is, in his opinion, an essential part of them. The same
general inference may be drawn from the fact that, among
the witnesses examined at the instance of the Association for
the Repeal of the Acts, there was no medical officer of either
service."

Again, with regard to the reduction of the disease among
the lower prostitutes, and the improvement in those localities
where the Acts have been in force, the commissioners speak
with no uncertain voice; and it is most instructive to
compare the following with the report of the committee
of 1862 :—*

"Soldiers and sailors under the influence of drink
are no longer importuned and seized upon by filthy prosti-

* See page 1.

tutes as they were in former days. It is true that the
ameliorated state of things is attributable, in some degree,
to causes independent of the Acts for prevention of contagious disease. The manners and habits of the people have
become generally much more decorous and wholesome during
the last generation, and this improvement has reached even
the degraded classes of society. It is not improbable that
the venereal contagion, like other diseases which are partly
engendered and always aggravated by neglect of cleanliness,
has been on the decline of late years. The various sanitary
regulations which have been enforced, and the increased
activity of the police in modern times, have all tended
to improve the public health. The Contagious Diseases
Acts, however, have both directly and indirectly promoted
the objects of sanitary and municipal police. *They have
purged the towns and encampments to which they have been
applied of miserable creatures who were mere masses of
rottenness and vehicles of disease,* providing them with
asylums where their sufferings could be temporarily relieved,
even if their malady was beyond cure, and where their better
nature was probably for the first time touched by human
sympathy."

But the alleviation of the physical sufferings of these
unfortunate women is not the only good that has accrued to
them from the Acts. The commissioners proceed in the next
paragraph (41) to say :—

"Although the reclamation of fallen women seems hardly
to have entered into the original conception of the Acts,
it soon became recognised as part of the system. A chaplain
is attached to each of the certified hospitals. The matrons
are mostly of a superior class, qualified by experience
for the performance of their duties, and animated by a
benevolent zeal for the work in which they are engaged.
The influences brought to bear upon the inmates of the

lock wards through these agencies are not without effect. Many of the women, on their discharge from the hospitals, have been induced to enter the refuges and homes which are ready for their reception."

The deterrent effects of the Acts are also alluded to, the commissioners remarking that they had had abundant evidence on this point. The evidence of the police, both special and local, is quoted, and the paragraph (43) concludes:—

"If such results have been attained, either wholly or partly, through the operation of the Acts, those who demand their absolute repeal are bound to show that they have produced evils to counterbalance the good which, after reasonable deductions have been made, may be fairly attributed to them."

.The question of the desirability of continuing the periodical examinations of all known prostitutes appears to have been the most difficult of any with which the commissioners had to deal; and it is, therefore, not surprising to find that they have endeavoured to make a compromise. In other words, they have tried to please everybody, supporters and repealers alike, with the usual result of pleasing nobody. They admit the fact that the examination of prostitutes, at regular and shortened periods, is the most effectual mode of dealing with venereal diseases, but they add, "It becomes a grave question whether the system could be maintained in the face of objections which on moral grounds have been raised against it." The tone of the report is apologetic; and there can be little doubt that in this matter the commissioners yielded to an agitated clamour raised by ignorant and prejudiced persons of both sexes. But, as will be seen, the whole tone of the report is favourable to the Acts, and entirely against repeal. They recommend that the periodical examinations be discontinued; that the Act of 1864 should be enforced, not only in the localities then under the protection of the Acts, but that its provisions should be "extended to any town in the United Kingdom which should make request for such extension, and should provide proper hospital accommodation for the reception of patients." They thus confirm considerably the recommendations of the Lords' and Commons' committees respectively.

With regard to what was urged by many witnesses, that on grounds of justice as expediency, soldiers and sailors should be subjected to regular examinations, they remark :— "We may at once dispose of this recommendation, so far as it is founded on the principle of putting both parties to the sin of fornication on the same footing by the obvious but not less conclusive reply, that there is no comparison to be made between prostitutes and the men who consort with them. With the one sex the offence is committed as a matter of gain ; with the other it is an irregular indulgence of a natural impulse." The argument that compelling prostitutes to enter a hospital, and detaining them there till cured, is an invasion of the liberty of the subject, is thus answered :— "We think, however, the temporary suspension of personal freedom, in this instance, such suspension being strictly measured by the time required to effect the patient's cure, and accompanied by no restraint unnecessary for such purpose, is not to be regarded as an infringement of a great constitutional principle."

In recommending that the Acts should be amended, the commissioners say :—"We attach great importance to the maintenance of a system, which, if it cannot altogether annul, may at least materially mitigate, a pestilence, which is not, like other contagions, of occasional occurrence, but one of perennial growth. The offenders who bring this affliction upon themselves by their own vicious indulgence may have no claim to the compassionate care of the State, but the numerous innocent persons who suffer from the disease are surely entitled to consideration. We venture to express our hope, therefore, that while due consideration is paid to the sentiments of the people with regard to prostitution, no misapprehension as to the real moral bearings of the question, and no want of courage, will be suffered to prevent the application of such remedy as may be practicable to this great evil. The firmness of a former Parliament withstood the storm of clamour with which the discovery of vaccination was assailed by the ignorance and prejudice of the day, and relieved posterity from a scourge which was the terror of former generations; and we would fain hope that the attempt to stay the progress of a plague scarcely less formidable in its ravages is not to be hastily abandoned." (Clause 64).

In their conclusion the commissioners object to the title of the Act as inapplicable to their proposed amended Act. They say:—" We do not recommend special legislation for the purpose of protecting from the consequences of vicious indulgence any class of your Majesty's servants; but we think that, for the public good, particular districts, which are from any cause peculiarly liable to contagious disease, should be subjected to special sanitary regulations. We therefore, approve of the establishment of hospitals at the public charge, and of police regulations, enforced under central authority within such districts. Having regard, however, to the general prevalence of the disease, and to its effects on the health and happiness of the innocent as well as the guilty, we are of opinion that such regulations should form part of a general measure comprising various amendments of the law."

It is by no means uncommon to find in the reports of Royal Commissions that the dissent is the most valuable part; and this remark certainly applies to the first dissent, which is signed by Lord Hampton, Viscount Hardinge, Sir J. Salusbury Trelawny, Bart., Drs. G. E. Paget and Wilks, Mr. Timothy Holmes, and Mr. G. W. Hastings. They thus give their reasons for dissenting from that part of the report which recommends that the periodical examinations of common prostitutes should be altogether given up, and that the Act of 1864 should be practically re-enacted :—

" We think the Act of 1864 is open to the serious objection, amongst others, that it gives discretionary powers to the police to lodge an information against any prostitute they ' have good cause to believe is diseased.' This is a dangerous power. The police might in some instances be over-zealous and active, in which case, complaint and dissatisfaction would arise; or probably more often they would be so cautious and careful as to whom they would accuse that little effect would be produced, and a great majority of cases of disease would escape detection.

" We have been, for these reasons, irresistibly led to the conclusion that it is only under a system of periodical examination that either venereal disease can be speedily detected and effectively checked, or police be safely entrusted with duties which must be admitted to be under the most favourable circumstances of a difficult and delicate nature, requiring every safeguard which prudence can suggest."

It is further suggested, and with great reason, " that the Act of 1866 had not been long enough in operation, even where first introduced, to admit of a fair judgment of its effects being formed."

The " good moral effects which these calumniated Acts have produced," are thus recapitulated :—

(A) Religious and moral influence has been brought to bear upon large numbers of women, a great portion of whom had been from infancy familiar only with scenes of debauchery and vice.

(*B*) Towns and camps have been cleared, or nearly so, of the miserable creatures who were formerly to be found in their streets and thoroughfares.

(*C*) A considerable number of abandoned women have been reclaimed and restored to respectable life, and in many instances married.

(*D*) The number of loose women has been greatly reduced, and those who remain have been rendered more decent and decorous in appearance and conduct.

(*E*) The practice of clandestine prostitution, which too often degenerates into professional vice, has been materially checked by fear of the consequences of such indulgence which are rendered probable under these Acts.

(*F*) The sad spectacle of juvenile prostitutes of tender age, so rife in such localities heretofore, has been greatly diminished ; in some instances almost removed.

(*G*) The temptations by which young men of all classes have been hitherto assailed, have been to a great extent taken out of their way, and morality has thus been promoted.

The seven commisioners we have named state, in conclusion :—

" We are of opinion that the total repeal of these Acts would be, as was said by a Devonport witness, ' disastrous.' We object to attempting a compromise, which would probably be unsuccessful, by retreating on an imperfect measure discredited by grave and obvious faults, and we desire to see the Acts of 1866 and 1869 maintained in substance and in principle."

Mr. Holmes further dissents from the clause which recommends extension of the Acts to the military districts of London, considering that nothing should be done to suggest that the Acts were intended for soldiers and sailors, and not for civilians. He also protests against the suggestion to subsidise voluntary hospitals, as unlikely to diminish the diseases, and as tending to increase the number of prostitutes.

Six of the commissioners, the Right Hon. W. Cowper-Temple, Mr. Mundella, M.P., the late Rev. J. F. D. Maurice, the late Mr. Holmes Coote, Mr. Applegarth, and Mr. Rylands dissent from the recommendation to re-enact the Act of 1864; and four of these gentlemen, in a further dissent, question the reduction of prostitutes and other good results of the Acts. The three other dissents, signed by Sir W. C. James, Bart., Mr. Buxton, and Dr. Bridges, respectively, give various objections to the re-enactments of the Act of 1864. It will be observed that only a very few of the commissioners were in favour of total repeal.

MEMORIAL IN SUPPORT OF THE ACTS, FROM 2,500 MEMBERS OF THE MEDICAL PROFESSION.

The report of the commission was issued in July, 1871. The complete exculpation of the police from the charges of abuse of authority laid against them; the almost unanimous recommendation that legislation on the subject should be continued; and the recognition of the principle of extension, were hailed with great satisfaction by the supporters of these Acts. But it was felt that the discontinuance of the compulsory periodical examinations would be a retrograde step, it being impossible to devise any sufficient substitute for them to secure satisfactory physical and moral results. The following letter was at first signed by the most eminent members of the medical profession in London, including all whose names I have already mentioned; copies were subsequently signed by most of the members of the profession in the towns subject to the Acts, and physicians and surgeons resident in London, Edinburgh, Dublin, and throughout the three kingdoms. In all, 2,500 signatures were obtained.

To the Right Hon. H. A. Bruce, M.P., Secretary of State
for the Home Department.

Sir,
Dec. 18, 1871.

We, the undersigned, beg to express to you the deep and continued interest we feel in the subject of legislation for the diminution of Contagious Venereal Disease.

Firmly convinced, as we are, of the deteriorating influence exercised by this form of disease on the public health, and painfully familiar with the serious suffering which it entails on large numbers of innocent individuals, we are most anxious that in any forthcoming measure nothing should be done to weaken the beneficial sanitary operation of the Acts at present in force, which can be shown to have reduced the more serious form of disease by considerably more than one-half in the districts where they are in operation. (*See the evidence of Dr. Balfour before the Royal Commission.*)

We especially wish to protest against the erroneous supposition that a personal examination is deemed by the women themselves either so degrading or repulsive as has been represented. We know, by long experience of this class, that they will flock in crowds to our public hospitals for admission, although the presence of a number of medical students render the exposure far greater than in the private chamber of an institution appropriated for this purpose by the Acts.

There is no difficulty in obtaining their voluntary attendance for even public examination when sick and incapable of further struggle with disease, but we know that, with rare exceptions, they cannot be induced to seclude themselves for treatment in the earlier and less painful stages of their complaints, when, for obvious reasons, they are most actively instrumental in communicating infection.

We therefore believe it to be absolutely essential to the success of any Act of the legislature on this subject, that it should provide effectually for the earliest possible detection and treatment of disease in public women, and we are unable to see how this can be accomplished otherwise than by a system of periodical examinations.

If then, Sir, we are warranted by recorded facts in our belief that the temporary seclusion of these diseased women in a more healthy moral atmosphere has been found to contribute, in no unimportant proportion of them, to their restitution to the paths of virtue; if, both physically and morally, they have been thereby raised in the scale of humanity, we trust you will not listen to a factitious opposition, founded on a most imperfect knowledge of the character and altered nature of these women, and of the extent of the evils to be remedied.

We conclude, Sir, with the expression of a most earnest hope that, in any future legislation on this subject, the main principles of the Acts of 1866 and 1869 may remain unaltered.

The Parliamentary Debates on the Motions to Repeal the Acts.

We have already seen that, in the session of 1870, the first motion for the repeal of the Contagious Diseases Acts was brought before the House of Commons, the debate being held with closed doors. Consequently, no report appeared in the newspapers, but the speech of the Right Hon. Dr. Lyon Playfair, M.P. for the Universities of Edinburgh and · St. Andrews, has been published. It contains several important facts not generally known, and which had, no doubt, a considerable impression on those who heard him. Thus, he stated that so "long ago as 1430 the Bishop of Winchester was charged by Ordinance with the regulation of eighteen houses of bad repute, which stood then and for centuries after on Bankside, Southwark." But, as the right honourable gentleman adds, "this did not give episcopal sanction to the sins committed in them." Again, remarking on the numerous petitions against the Acts that emanated from Scotland, principally on the grounds of interference with the liberty of the subject, he reminds his countrymen that the credit or discredit of having found out how to arrest these contagious diseases rests with them. "In the year 1497 the Aberdeen magistrates shrewdly suspected that the disease was not an epidemic, and they ordered all diseased women to abandon their evil courses, and shut themselves up in their houses till they were cured, branding on the cheek with a red hot key those who came out too soon. And six months later the Privy Council ordered the magistrates

and town council of Edinburgh to collect all diseased
women, along with their doctors, on the sands of Leith,
boats being provided to transport them to the island of
Inchkeith, where they were to remain till cured, on pain of
being branded in a like way. Really, the north should not be
so hard on its gentler southern progeny." In his conclusion,
Dr. Playfair says :—" For three and a half centuries these
diseases have been the scandal of civilisation, and neither
philanthropy nor religion have stopped their growth. It
is long since Parliament has known the serious character of
the disease. In the year 1529 it arraigned Cardinal Wolsey
for daring to go into the presence of the king while he was
afflicted with it, when he ought to have isolated himself from
one in whom the State was interested. This enforced isola-
tion of diseased persons we now extend to the forces which
are kept up for the protection of the State. For three and a
half years this active policy of prevention has substituted the
do-nothing policy of three and a half centuries, and the result
has been largely to mitigate disease, and to lessen immorality. I trust, therefore, that the House will not repeal
Acts when their past history has answered our expectations,
and while their future is full of promise."

The second motion for the repeal of the Acts was brought
forward by Mr. Fowler, on the 22nd May, 1873. Lord
Hampton (then Sir John Pakington) moved, as an amendment, that the Bill be read that day six months, which was
seconded by Mr. J. D. Lewis, the late member for Devonport, in an admirable speech, which has also been published,
and which concludes in these trenchant words :—" Sir, in
conclusion, let me assure the House that the agitation on
this subject is slowly, but surely, dying out. It was always
loudest, or perhaps I should rather say shrillest, in proportion to the distance of the persons who raised it, and the
localities where they lived, from the places where the Acts

were practically known and appreciated. It was never greater than that which was raised against vaccination, on its first introduction, by old women of both sexes. But the House of Commons of that day stood firm, and I trust that the House of Commons of this day will stand equally firm, and not proceed to decree the unrestricted circulation of venereal poison to the detriment of posterity, whose curses we should incur, and, what is worse, we should merit. I trust there will be no successful efforts to tamper with these Acts, which in localities where they have been in force have done more in a few short years to alleviate one of the most frightful scourges which can afflict humanity, to improve the condition of the towns, to eradicate juvenile prostitution, to bring to bear a moral influence on the unfortunate women who are subject to them, than all the voluntary efforts of all the philanthropists who have ever existed." The motion was lost by a majority of 123 ; 128 voting in favour, 251 against. To the great indignation of many members, " strangers were spied," and the press excluded.

On the 23rd June, 1875, Sir Harcourt Johnstone moved the repeal of the Acts, and for the first time the debate on a motion for repeal was in an open House, full reports being published in the *Times* and other daily papers. An amendment to the effect that the Bill be read that day three months was moved by Colonel Alexander, and carried by a majority of 182 ; 126 voting for the repeal, 308 for the amendment. Thus, for the third time, and by a considerably increased majority, the House of Commons decided that these Acts shall not be repealed, confirming the recommendations of their Select Committee, of that of the House of Lords, and of the Royal Commissioners. It would, indeed, be strange if it were otherwise, and a perusal of the debate will show that those in favour of the Acts had, in addition to numbers, reason, right, and sound common sense on their side. On the other hand, the opponents of the Acts brought forward nothing new, only the old objections, now worn thread-bare, all of which were completely met and confuted.

THE QUESTION NOT A POLITICAL ONE.

A very slight glance will show this. The first Act was passed during the Government of the late Lord Palmerston, in 1864 ; the second, that of 1866, was brought in by the Right Hon. H. C. E. Childers (as he acknowledged during the debate) ; the third Act was passed in 1869, during the late Administration. The medical memorial was presented to Mr. Bruce (then the Home Secretary) by a deputation, consisting of a hundred and fifty members of Parliament, composed equally of Conservatives and Liberals. The first two motions for repeal were brought forward during the late, the third and last during the present Government. Politicians of both sides are to be found among the supporters and opponents of the Acts, and this, from the very nature of the subject, is what we might expect. This much, however, is quite clear, that the majority of members of the House of Commons are opposed to the repeal of these Acts ; and, subject to the improvements which may from time to time be suggested and acted upon, in favour of their retention on the statutes. The opposition still continues, and has so far prevented their extension, though only for a season. The supporters of these Acts may, however, console themselves with the saying of Talleyrand : " The thoughts of the greatest number of intelligent persons, in any time or country, are sure, with a few fluctuations, more or less, to become in the end the public opinion of their age or community."

THE REPEAL TO BE AGAIN MOVED.

Notice has been given again of a Bill to repeal the Acts, the second reading of which stands for July 19th. I propose to discuss the matter in a very practical way, by giving some particulars respecting prostitution and venereal diseases in this large town, and comparing these with similar details in places where the Acts are in force. It will confirm what is stated in the following paragraph of the last report of the Association for Promoting the Extension of these Acts, which, I trust, may receive some attention at the forthcoming debate:—

" Under present circumstances, we do not aim at so wide and immediate an extension of the Acts as before, but the case of certain seaport towns not subject to the Acts, which are known to be hotbeds of disease introduced by sailors of the merchant service of our own and of foreign countries, is so glaring, and is attended with such disastrous consequences, that we feel it our duty to call for the special interference of Parliament to repress the evil."

We shall also be able to answer, in some measure, the questions put at the commencement of this Paper : Are these maladies (*i. e.*, venereal diseases,) on the increase? Are they undergoing any modification in their type? I shall endeavour to confine myself as much as possible to facts, and only such figures and statistics as may be easily understood. I have no wish to add another to the many reproaches which have been cast upon my native town, which we still call the "good old town," in spite of all the abuse that has lately been levelled at it. My object is to show that the evils of prostitution (especially the diseases resulting directly and indirectly from it) in our large mercantile seaports cannot be dealt with by ordinary police regulations and voluntary hospital accommodation ; and I select, naturally, that seaport with which I am most acquainted.

EXTENT AND POPULATION OF LIVERPOOL.

The first seaport of the world is so well known that it is only necessary for me to notice those circumstances which determine the prevalence of prostitution and its attendant evils. The borough of Liverpool extends 4·7 miles in length, from north to south; in breadth, from east to west, 2·3 miles. Within the area thus enclosed is a population now estimated at 520,000, the rapidly-increasing nature of which may be judged from the following census returns :—

1831	...	..	165,221
1841		...	293,963
1851	...	...	376,065
1861		...	462,749
1871	...	... ...	493,346

There is a very large floating and ever-changing population, and from forty to fifty thousand may be reckoned as the number of seamen constantly in port, all of the mercantile marine. This is subject to great variations at times, as a fair wind may bring in as many as a hundred and fifty vessels in one day, while, after a period of unfavourable weather, a like number may leave the port. Next to London, there is no place which contains more young persons of both sexes sent to make their way; and I may here remark, that among the mercantile marine and civil population generally are many persons who are practically quite as much debarred from marriage as soldiers, or sailors in the navy. I do not state this as any justification for prostitution, far from it; but I state it, as determining its existence and prevalence, as a fact. The average merchant seaman receives from 50s. to 60s. per month in wages, subject to certain deductions. Supposing that he allotted half or even three-fourths of this, it is little more than will suffice for the bare existence of a wife, even without incumbrances. I pass over the many other drawbacks and discomforts which any woman marrying a sailor must encounter; it is quite sufficient to state that, except in a few cases, marriage is, for the average merchant seaman, out of the question; he must wait till he have attained some higher grade in his calling. And as hundreds and even thousands of seamen live and die without ever getting higher than " before the mast," it follows, as a matter of course, that in every large seaport there will be a number of seamen practically compelled to lead a celibate life, a number quite equal to that of a very large garrison, or the crews of many men-of-war. In such a state of matters, prostitution will always be found, and this is certainly the case in Liverpool.

EXTENT OF PROSTITUTION IN LIVERPOOL.

The following very elaborate Tables are extracted from the last report of Major Greig, C.B., Head Constable, for the year ending 29th September, 1875.

These, I need hardly observe, are only the numbers of prostitutes well known to the police, the great majority of whom, it will be observed, reside in brothels. The north, south, and east boundaries of this borough are very arbitrary, being in many parts defined by the middle of a street, one side being in the borough, the other in the adjoining out-township of West Derby, Toxteth, or Walton, and under the control of the county police. Hence, many women who undoubtedly practise prostitution in the borough reside beyond its boundaries, and are not included in the above returns. This also accounts, to a great extent, for the reduction in the numbers during the past six years. It will be observed that there has been a great reduction in the numbers both of brothels and prostitutes since the year 1870. In that year the state of the streets attracted the serious attention of the magistrates and police authorities; for a long time they had been remarkably free from solicitation and other evils attendant on prostitution, but six years ago the evil again became rather prominent. Vigorous measures were adopted, and the appearance of the streets is greatly

C

TABLE No. 11.—GIVES THE NUMBER OF BROTHELS AND PROSTITUTES KNOWN TO THE POLICE, ALSO THE NUMBER OF HOUSES OF ACCOMMODATION, HOUSES WHERE PROSTITUTES LODGE, ALSO A COMPARATIVE STATEMENT OF BROTHELS AND PROSTITUTES FOR TEN YEARS.

DIVISIONS.	Brothels known to the Police kept by		Houses of Accommodation.	Houses where Prostitutes Lodge, not Brothels.	Number of Prostitutes.	Males residing in Brothels.	RETURN OF BROTHELS FOR TEN YEARS.										RETURN OF PROSTITUTES FOR TEN YEARS.									
	Males.	Females.					1866	1867	1868	1869	1870	1871	1872	1873	1874	1875	1866	1867	1868	1869	1870	1871	1872	1873	1874	1875
North Town	23	256	17	18	696	51	302	392	416	421	423	363	242	298	241	279	1248	1059	1158	1172	1266	990	584	857	619	696
South Town	19	153	9	13	441	15	425	453	353	399	407	305	223	218	217	172	974	1417	1061	1077	1184	732	646	524	637	441
TOTAL....	42	409	26	31	1137	66	727	845	789	820	830	668	465	516	458	451	2222	2476	2219	2249	2450	1722	1230	1381	1256	1137

improved. The following extract from Major Greig's comments on the same Table (No. 11), in his report for 1874, shows the instructions on which the police act, and also accounts for the decrease in brothels :—

" Table No. 11 gives the number of brothels and prostitutes known to the police, also a comparative statement for ten years. Formerly the census was taken, in accordance with instructions from the Home Office, on the first Tuesday in April; but as these classes of houses and persons are now struck out of the Government return, this return was not made until September 29, and only relates to the prostitutes known to the police (exclusive of those in gaol) to be within the borough on that night. Brothels, 458; prostitutes, 1,256—a decrease in the former of 58, and in the latter of 125. This decrease may be accounted for by the removal of many persons keeping houses of this class from streets in the vicinity of West Derby-road. The memorandum of instructions, issued in 1871, respecting this class of houses, has continued to be strictly carried out, proceedings having been taken in most cases ' where young girls were kept, or robberies were committed, where they were of notoriously bad character and had become a public nuisance, where they were opened in a respectable street or leading thoroughfare, and where they were complained of by two or more of the inhabitants of the street, who were prepared to substantiate their complaints in court.' Many of the keepers of these houses have been removed by the police, and others on complaint by the inhabitants, without the necessity of proceedings being taken in the police-court."

Commenting on another Table in the same report, Major Greig says :—

"Table No. 12 gives the number of prostitutes taken into custody and summarily convicted ; 2,379 persons, 6,033 arrests ; 1,776 persons convicted, and 4,345 convictions. A large proportion of these were taken into custody under the Vagrant Act, and charged with being idle and disorderly. This has conduced to better order in our great thoroughfares."

I have thought it necessary to give these explanations, as a perusal of the above might lead to the inference that the number of prostitutes in Liverpool at the present time is less than half of what it was in 1870, an inference which I feel satisfied cannot be supported for a moment. The police returns include only notorious prostitutes, and mostly of a very low class, on a certain day; and I feel convinced that we shall never know the full extent of prostitution, except under a special police. The circumstances which favour prostitution have not diminished, but rather increased, of late years; and, considering the relative numbers in other towns where, under a special police, full and accurate returns were obtainable, I should estimate the number of prostitutes in Liverpool at from two to three thousand. But the number known to the police, which, for convenience, we will take as 1,200, is sufficiently large to suggest serious reflections, and will afford a very good *minimum* number on which to base calculations.

PROSTITUTION IN THE LOWER PARTS OF THE TOWN.
"*Blackman's Alley.*"

We have already seen what strong terms were applied by the Special Committee of 1862, and the Royal Commissioners, in describing the prostitutes surrounding the sailors' homes in Portsmouth, Devonport, Plymouth, and elsewhere, prior to the commencement of the Acts. It could hardly be expected that any great amelioration from such state will be found in this and other seaports, where large numbers of merchant seamen, both English and foreign, are to be found. The women who practise prostitution among them are not likely to be superior to their fallen sisters in naval ports ; and I feel sure that a committee appointed to inquire into the prevalence of venereal disease in the mercantile marine service would use terms quite as strong as the committee of 1862. Having had medical charge of three different parochial districts in the lower parts of this town, I am in a position to speak with some authority on the state of the brothels and prostitutes in them. In one district, situated in the northern part of the town, there is a region, comprising several streets of considerable length, known by various names, the least objectionable, perhaps, of which is "Blackman's Alley." These streets contain a large number of brothels of the very lowest class, the male frequenters being the numerous negroes who act as stewards, cooks, and seamen on board the numerous vessels arriving in the Mersey, and thus give its name to this locality. The female inmates of these dens of infamy are chiefly those who are the most virtuous in their own country, viz., Irish girls. They do not crouch behind the bushes, as did the "wrens of the Curragh," nor do they burrow in the ground, nor hide in ditches, as did the women at Aldershot, for the obvious reason that none of these acts are possible, there being no bushes, nor ditches, nor ground, except that covered with flags or "square sets." But the moral and social condition of these poor creatures is not one whit less degraded, nor their physical state less diseased, than those alluded to. The terms, "mere masses of rottenness and vehicles of disease," would, I feel sure, be quite as applicable to them as to the women formerly found in Devonport, Portsmouth, or any of the other seaports which now have the benefit of the Acts. I have myself, on several occasions, seen one of these unfortunates crouched in a corner of the room, unable to move, begging to be removed to the workhouse hospital.

Some few find their way to the Lock Hospital; others, when unable any longer to continue prostitution, not in consequence of disease, but in consequence of the physical suffering it causes, are admitted into the workhouse hospital. But their admission is the same as that of other paupers, viz., through the relieving officer; and the slightest acquaintance with our parochial system must convince anyone that it can never be relied on to materially diminish either the prevalence or severity of syphilis. It is true that, under the Act 30 and 31 Vict., cap. 106, sec. 22, the authorities of the workhouse have power to detain compulsorily, till cured, any paupers afflicted with contagious disease; and it has been decided that this includes venereal disease. I am also able to say that this is rigidly enforced in all the local workhouses. But the mischief which has been done, both to the patient and others, long before she seeks admission either to the voluntary hospital or workhouse, is quite inconceivable, except by those who see her[1] on her arrival there. A large proportion, however, of the lower prostitutes in this town, as in London and elsewhere, resort to the dispensaries, or to chemists and druggists in their neighbourhood; and I am sorry to say that the following extract from a Paper by the late Mr. Acton describes most accurately what may be seen every night in this town :—

"It is now many years ago since I called public attention to the error committed by philanthropists and medical men in treating prostitutes as out-patients. I regret to say that what I wrote and published, regarding our civil hospital arrangements, twelve years ago, applies equally at the present day (1870). I, however, now go farther, and venture to question whether it is desirable for our civil hospitals to treat prostitutes as out-patients at all.

"Every man who frequents the street, after nightfall, must meet many a woman, apparently sound and healthy, who,

patched up by voluntary charity in the morning, knows
no other way—nay, whose only possible resource—to get her
necessary food, or bed at night, than to sally forth into the
streets. The ministers of charity may have eased her pain
in the morning, dressed her sores and given her drugs, but
in a month she will be no nearer soundness than had she
been taken care of by the State within the walls of the hospital for one week; and within that month what a scourge upon
society will the surgeons not have kept afoot by their exertions?
Here is the power of charity again working to waste."

In the south-west part of the town is the Sailors' Home,
where a large number of sailors constantly reside. Close by
are the offices of the Mercantile Marine Board, where crews
are paid off; and, as might be expected, a considerable
number of public-houses and low brothels are in close
proximity. There are several streets here only differing from
those in "Blackman's Alley" in that they are more frequented thoroughfares, and therefore comparatively more
decent; but their inhabitants are of a similar class. No
description could convey any idea of the sights and scenes to
be witnessed here; it is appalling to those whose professional
duties might have been expected to render them hardened
to such. I gladly follow the example of the committee
of 1862, and refrain from further details. I would only
repeat my conviction that a Parliamentary committee would
describe in similar, or even stronger, terms the mass of vice
filth and disease which surrounds the merchant seamen's
Homes, and would with equal strength press upon the
present Government the necessity of at once grappling with
it. We have heard much lately of unseaworthy ships;
but it is time that some of the energy and zeal which
have been displayed with regard to the ships should be
extended to the crews, who are surely of more importance,

and, I fear, very often equally unseaworthy with the worst.
The hard-earned wages of a long voyage are in a few
short days spent in the lowest of gin-palaces, with the
lowest of prostitutes ; the merchant seaman ships again for
another long voyage ; there is (as a general rule) no medical
inspection to see if he is free from disease, as this is
optional, not compulsory ; and it is well known, in this and
other seaports, that many vessels are weak-handed within a
few days after leaving port, in consequence of the infection
of the crews with venereal disease. Nor is this all ; the
medical treatment of such cases on board ship is obviously
very imperfect, as the majority of vessels leaving this port
carry no surgeon. The infected seamen thus frequently
carry their disease with them to foreign ports, arriving there
with constitutions thoroughly tainted with the disease ; or, if
it should be of a milder form, propagating it there. That
this is no over-drawn picture can be amply testified by
medical practitioners in this and other ports, while we shall
have collateral proof further on.

In the more central parts of this town there are several
streets containing many brothels of a somewhat less
degraded class, but where much disease prevails. A map of
Liverpool, with the various streets where well-known brothels
are marked in it, shows that, while they are congregated
in certain localities, they are to be found spread all over the
town and in the adjacent suburbs. The last thirty years
have produced many changes; and streets which were
formerly the abode of the gentry, or even the aristocracy, of
Liverpool, have become merged into the " slums."

What is the Probable Ratio of Disease among the Prostitutes of this Town ?

Though this cannot be accurately ascertained till periodical inspection of all known prostitutes is enforced, we may

arrive at some approximation to the truth by observing what was the ratio in those ports where the Acts are now in force, at the time of their first introduction. Under the Act of 1864, only such prostitutes as were suspected of being diseased were brought up for examination ; and the care with which this was done may be judged from the fact that, in Portsmouth, out of 331 women, 294 were found diseased, or 88·82 per cent. ; while, in Devonport, 202 women were all found to be diseased. In Dover, the periodical inspection of all known prostitutes was commenced in 1870, and, out of 202 women, 52, or 25·74 per cent., were found diseased. In Gravesend, the ratio was 21·49 ; in Southampton, 34·70. Considering the frightful severity of the disease in the women seen at the dispensaries, in the Lock Hospital, in the lock wards of the Liverpool Parish Infirmary, and of the West Derby and Toxteth workhouses ; taking the numbers into consideration, and comparing them with the hospital admissions in the above ports, I am satisfied that a ratio of 40 per cent. is not at all excessive, and that at least that proportion of the prostitutes in this town would be found infected with venereal disease.

We have seen that there are known to the police, in round numbers, *1,200* prostitutes. This would, at a ratio of 40 per cent., give *480* as the number of diseased prostitutes to be found plying their trade in this town. If, however, I am correct in supposing that this is the minimum, and that there are at least double that number of prostitutes, we reach a figure of *960*.

HOSPITAL ACCOMMODATION FOR VENEREAL DISEASES IN LIVERPOOL.

The only voluntary hospital we possess is the lock hospital of the Royal Infirmary, the history of which is both interesting and instructive.

In the year 1745, the population of Liverpool being about 25,000, the Royal Infirmary (the first medical charity) was established; and its founders, observing that this was then a rising seaport, with a large maritime population, and, taking a liberal and large-hearted view of their duties, admitted all kinds of diseases, including venereal. When, in 1824, the present Infirmary was erected; two wards were set apart in it for male, two for female venereal patients, these four wards containing an aggregate of nearly fifty beds. Later on, when more room was required, the committee decided to place all venereal cases in a separate building, and with a separate staff, and the present lock hospital was accordingly erected in 1834, with a total of fifty beds, twenty-five for each sex. The greatest credit is due to the committee of the Royal Infirmary for thus establishing and maintaining this most useful institution, in spite of difficulties which would scarcely be credited. The charge made against the originators and supporters of these Acts, of providing clean women for vicious men, was urged many years ago as a reason for closing this hospital; and it is very evident that but for the circumstance of the first hospital in this town admitting cases of venereal disease, we should, in all probability, be at this present moment without any lock hospital at all. The accommodation (fifty beds) remains the same; and, seeing that the two hospitals, the Royal Infirmary and Lock Hospital together, contain an aggregate of 320 beds, the proportion of 50 beds, nearly one-sixth, is very liberal, and is, in fact, larger than in any metropolitan hospital. It is, therefore, not to be expected that the committee of the Royal Infirmary should, unaided, provide further accommodation. When the hospital was first erected, the population of Liverpool was one-third of what it is now; and we may assume that the fifty beds were provided for the present and not the future generation. Since that date, three general hospitals—the

Northern, Royal Southern, and Stanley—have been established, with an aggregate of 364 beds ; but in none of these are any set apart for these contagious diseases. A few males, such as foreign seamen and others, are admitted, on payment of a weekly sum, in the Royal Southern Hospital ; some cases of tertiary syphilis are admitted into the Northern Hospital ; a considerable number of these cases are treated as out-patients at the Stanley Hospital ; but the number of beds set apart for cases of venereal disease remains the same as in 1834, viz., 25 beds for male, 25 for female, patients. It is the old story, "What is everybody's business is nobody's business," with the old result, that nobody attends to it.

But, after all, we are better off than many of our neighbours in this respect; and I would here beg for a careful perusal of the various returns in the Appendix,* which I have prepared with great labour and care, and after a considerable correspondence with the various medical officers (honorary and resident) of the numerous hospitals given, to whom I take this opportunity of tendering my sincere thanks. We have heard much of lock hospitals on the voluntary system, and lock wards in general hospitals on the voluntary principle. I think a perusal of these returns will convince all reasonable people that a more correct term would be the "voluntary want of system," or the "unsystematic principle." It will be seen that, in one hospital, male patients are only admitted on payment, while females are admitted free ; and that in another hospital exactly the reverse of this obtains. On what principle are the number of beds determined ? Why should Glasgow have between 60 and 70 beds in its Lock Hospital ; Dublin 150, all for females ; and Liverpool, which is at least equal to,

* See pages 82 to 85.

if not larger than, the first, and double the size of the second, only 25 ?

Many other striking anomalies will be apparent, but further comment is needless, and fault-finding with benevolent institutions is ungracious work.

HAVE VENEREAL DISEASES LATELY DIMINISHED IN FREQUENCY AND SEVERITY IN LIVERPOOL ?

It is not so easy to answer this question as might at first appear, but this much may be said *in limine*, that here, as well as throughout the kingdom, these diseases have always been much more prevalent than the general public have been willing to believe. Because lock hospitals and lock wards are in this country few and far between, and with very limited accommodation, whilst continental towns and cities have large hospitals, with ample provision for these diseases, many people have concluded that they are rife on the continent and rare in England. It would be as logical to infer that in those countries where there are no lunatic asylums, there are no persons of unsound mind ; or that in country districts where there is no hospital, fractured limbs are not to be found ; or that localities which possess no lifeboat, are free from shipwrecks. So long ago as the sixteenth century, this erroneous idea would appear to have been prevalent, as is seen in the following quaint extract from a medical publication of that period :—

" If I be not deceived in mine opinion (friendly reader), I suppose the disease itselfe was never more rife in Naples, Italie, France, or Spaine, than it is this day in the Realme of England. I may speake boldly because I speake truly ; and yet I speake it with griefe of minde that in the Hospital of Saint Bartholomew, in London, there hath been cured of this disease, by me and three others, within five years, to the number of one thousand and more. I speake nothing of

Saint Thomas Hospital, and other houses about the citie, wherein an infinite multitude are daily cured. *It happened very seldom in the Hospitall of Saint Bartholomew's whilst I stayed there, amongst every twenty diseased that were taken into the said house, which was most commonly on the Monday, ten of them were infected with Lues Venerea."—A brief and necessary Treatise tovching the cvre of the disease now vsvally called Lves Venerea*, by W. Clovves, one of her Maiesties Chirurgions, 1596, p. 149.

I have already stated that I only intend to give such figures and statistics as may be easily understood. The following is a return of the admissions into the Liverpool Lock Hospital, for the sixteen years, 1860 to 1875, both inclusive :—

YEAR.	Males.	Females.	Total.	YEAR.	Males.	Females.	Total.
1860	233	158	391	1868....	248	164	412
1861	276	200	476	1869....	309	206	515
1862	284	198	482	1870....	366	196	562
1863	284	216	500	1871....	316	153	469
1864	294	222	516	1872....	281	150	431
1865	227	158	385	1873....	298	185	483
1866	279	158	437	1874....	312	144	456
1867	255	177	432	1875....	295	172	467

The extraordinary and persistent preponderance of males over females will at once be apparent, being the reverse of what is, I believe, the rule elsewhere.* The number of males would be far more, but for the limited accommodation. Had

* Since writing the above, I find that a similar preponderance exists in the Bristol Workhouse.

we fifty instead of twenty-five beds on the men's side of the hospital, I feel sure that we could keep them fairly filled all the year round. On the other side, that allotted to females, I regret to say that we have seldom more than half the beds occupied.

In the Liverpool Parish Infirmary, many cases of venereal disease are treated, and by the kindness of Dr. Alexander, the present visiting surgeon, I have been enabled to see the wards. I am indebted to Mr. Hagger, the vestry clerk, and Mr. Wilkie, the governor of the workhouse, for the following :—

LIVERPOOL PARISH INFIRMARY.

LOCK WARDS.

Return of Paupers admitted with Venereal Disease.

YEAR.	Males.	Females.	Total.	YEAR.	Males.	Females.	Total.
1865	240	190	430	1870	241	213	454
1866	253	198	451	1871	191	167	358
1867	288	204	492	1872	157	142	299
1868	209	175	384	1873	202	196	398
1869	208	257	465	1874	182	213	395
				1875	123	186	309

With a few exceptions, the same preponderance of male over female patients is to be noticed, and this of itself would show these diseases to be very prevalent in this town, the more so as the greater proportion of the above are very severe cases, as we shall presently see.

There are also lock wards in the West Derby Union and Toxteth Workhouse Infirmaries, but I have been able to procure only the returns of the last few years :—

41

WEST DERBY UNION INFIRMARY.

Number of Patients admitted into the Lock Wards.

YEAR.	Males.	Females.	Total.	YEAR.	Males.	Females.	Total.
1871	27	34	61	1873	16	33	49
1872	14	16	30	1874	18	22	40

TOXTETH WORKHOUSE INFIRMARY.

YEAR ENDING JULY.	Males.	Females.	Total.	YEAR ENDING JULY.	Males.	Females.	Total.
1872	2	13	15	1874	4	18	22
1873	5	10	15	1875	5	17	22

* It will be observed, that whilst there are considerable fluctuations in the different years, there is no real diminution in the numbers. So far, then, as the primary affections treated in the above institutions would show, these diseases have not decreased in frequency of late years.

At the three Dispensaries, many patients suffering from syphilis in all its forms, and a very large number of cases of gonorrhœa, are seen. At the Infirmary for Children, many cases of infantile syphilis are seen among the out-patients. At the Eye and Ear Infirmary, many diseases of syphilitic origin are also seen. I am not, however, able to give any reliable statistics of these, for reasons which will be obvious to all who have the medical charge of out-patients. To enter accurately in any out-patients' register those cases which are syphilitic, is a work of great difficulty. This is especially the case when the diseases are general; when special, the diagnosis may not be positive (as to the syphilitic origin of

* Compare the above returns with those on page 53 postea.

the disease) for some time after the patient's first appearance.

But we have a very striking and sad proof of the prevalence and fatality of this disease among children by the following returns, which I have extracted from the annual reports of Dr. Trench, the Medical Officer of Health :—

Deaths from Syphilis in Liverpool.

Year.	Males.	Females.	Total.	Infants under 1 year.
1860	.. 37	... 31	... 68	... 51
1861	... 33	... 30	... 63	... 48
1862	... 36	... 43	... 79	... 64
1863	... 42	... 34	... 76	... 64
1864	... 38	42	.. 80	... 70
1865	47	... 41	... 88	... 75
1866	... 49	... 45	... 94	... 79
1867	... 43	... 38	... 81	... 72
1868	... 55	... 49	... 104	... 91
1869	... 29	... 37	... 66	... 51
1870	... 62	... 45	... 107	... 92
1871	... 50	... 47	... 97	... 89
1872	. 50	36	... 86	... 71
1873	... 39	... 39	... 78	... 63
1874	... 50	... 42	... 92	77
1875	.. 42	... 28	... 70	... 60

It must not be supposed that these are by any means the total numbers of deaths from this disease. The certificate of death given by medical practitioners is not forwarded in confidence to the registrar of deaths, but is given to the person who asks for it, who may be the father, mother, or other near relative of the deceased. The meaning of the word *syphilis* is now pretty well known, hence a great reluctance on the part of practitioners to certify to such being the cause of death, or, indeed, to introduce the ominous abbreviation *syph.* into the certificate at all. Consequently, many deaths

are returned annually as from bronchitis, pneumonia, etc.,
which are really due to syphilis. I may here quote, as con-
firmatory of this, so high an authority as Sir W. Jenner,
who, in his evidence before the Lords' Committee, in answer
to the question, "What is your experience with reference to
the prevalence of constitutional syphilis among children at
those hospitals?" (Hospital for Sick Children and University
College Hospital) states:—

"That it is exceedingly prevalent, and that it leads to a
very large number of deaths annually *which do not appear as
deaths from syphilis* in the Registrar-General's return, but as
deaths from secondary disease."

The real number of deaths of infants below one year due
to syphilis within this borough, is probably double or treble
the above, and, considering that this is a perfectly preventible
disease, I think this annual destruction of children's lives
calls for very serious consideration.

A very large proportion of venereal disease occuring in
this town among the lower, as well as the middle and upper
classes, comes before the notice of private practitioners. The
restricted hours between which hospital out-door and dispensary patients are seen, excludes a large number. From
inquiries I have made among practitioners in different parts
of this town, who are so circumstanced as to see many of
such cases, and from general observations, I am satisfied that
there is no diminution in their frequency, as seen in private
practice. If, too, the number of advertising quacks may be
taken as a criterion of the prevalence of this disease, as I fear
it must, we have still stronger proof, since these harpies
flourish and abound, especially near the Sailors' Home,
where many a poor sailor is allured by their promises of a
speedy cure and low fees, neither of which is fulfilled.

As regards the severity of syphilis, I will first give the

opinions of those local practitioners who have had long and extensive experience in this department of surgery, and whose opinions are entitled to respect. Mr. Worthington, Consulting Surgeon to the Lock Hospital, who speaks from an experience of upwards of forty years, informs me that he sees no diminution either in the frequency or severity of syphilis. My colleague, Mr. McCheane, speaking from twenty-four years' experience, sees no diminution either in its prevalence or severity. On the other hand, Mr. Chauncy Puzey, who was surgeon to the hospital for about two years, tells me that the cases he saw there are less severe than those he saw in the venereal wards of Guy's Hospital, fourteen years ago. The severity of the cases in our hospital strikes all practitioners who have never seen it before, or not for some years past. It is now fourteen years since I attended the hospital as a student, for a period of nearly two years, and took particular notice of the cases which passed through. I only visited occasionally till my appointment as surgeon, more than twelve months ago, and my own impression is, that while there are certainly fewer cases of sloughing or phagedenic sores, involving loss or mutilation of the genital organs, syphilis, in its primary, secondary, and tertiary form, is quite as severe and frequent as it was then. The greater proportion of the patients now admitted suffer from constitutional syphilis, and the students of the Liverpool Royal Infirmary School of Medicine, who are permitted to attend the practice, have almost unrivalled opportunities of studying this disease in all its varieties. So long as it exists to the extent I have described, it is very desirable that students should possess such facilities. I trust, however, that as the students of a former generation had the opportunity of witnessing the gradual diminution and almost total extinction of small-pox, the students of the present generation may witness the gradual extinction of this most loathsome and even fatal disease. The male wards of our hospital are constantly full; patients who go out cured are at once replaced by severe cases, and as many as thirty men have been sent away in a week for want of room. On the female side, we have to regret that even the limited accommodation is not availed of as we might expect, when we know that so much disease prevails; half the beds are generally empty, though I have no hesitation in stating that in the localities I have described,* a single street would furnish a sufficient number of suitable candidates, in the shape of diseased prostitutes, to fill every one of the twenty-five beds. The hospital has always been under the most excellent management, and every kindness and consideration is shown to the patients by the able and courteous superintendent and matron, Mr. and Mrs. Serjeant. They are admitted without any difficulty, the only requirement being, that they shall be provided with a sufficiency of clean linen. They come in when they please, and the appearance of most on admission shows considerable neglect, and want of the most ordinary cleanliness; and as we have no power to compel them to stay, they can leave whenever they wish. I am glad to say that, with few exceptions, they stay till they are well; but it is very disheartening to see at times several leaving at once, very far from cured, who, on returning to their vocation, must spread disease to a considerable extent. The majority of the patients are of course prostitutes, often very young, and their average stay in hospital is from five to six weeks. It is much to be hoped that soon some arrangement may be made to afford a classification of the patients, so that young girls who have only just commenced a life of profligacy may be separated from older prostitutes, and married women, who have been infected by their husbands, from either.

As showing the difference between voluntary and compul-

* See page 31, ante.

sory treatment in lessening the severity of disease in women, I may here quote the words of Mr. James R. Lane, Surgeon to the London Lock Hospital, who, writing in 1870, says :—

"The good effect of legislative supervision in gradually lessening the *severity* of the disease, does not admit of numerical expression ; the alteration in its quality, however, is quite as strongly marked as the diminution in quantity, and is of equal, if not greater, importance. The severe and shocking cases which are so frequently seen in the wards of voluntary lock hospitals, are almost unknown in the hospitals receiving patients under these Acts. The more important form of disease, viz., syphilis, soon becomes singularly mild in character, and quickly amenable to treatment, both in its primary and secondary manifestations ; while a considerable majority of the patients now admitted are suffering solely from the milder form of disease, or gonorrhœa. I can testify to this from personal observation at the London Lock Hospital, where women have been received under the Contagious Diseases Acts since the passing of the first Act in 1864. When patients are first admitted from a new district, the cases are quite equal in severity to those which I am accustomed to see in the voluntary wards of the same hospital, and nothing can be more striking than the alteration which takes place in this respect after a district has been for six months subjected to compulsory inspection. This is a fact of great interest, and tells strongly in favour of the system ; it is one of which even those who have interested themselves in the results of these Acts are not yet, I think, sufficiently aware."

The cases seen at the Liverpool Parish Infirmary, and the other workhouses, are also of a very severe kind. There is always delay on the part of women seeking admission, partly because they must apply as paupers, partly from unwillingness to enter hospital. It seems to me also that

now that the authorities of workhouses have power to detain
till cured all suffering from contagious diseases, this probably
acts as a deterrent to their entering. Dr. Alexander, however, does not think that such is the case, and a perusal of
the returns * would appear to confirm this.

Mr. Lane has so ably described the advantages of compulsory over voluntary treatment, that I cannot do better
than give his own words :—

" The alternative proposed by many of those who object
to the Contagious Diseases Acts is an increased number of
lock hospitals to which patients should be admitted on the
voluntary system. I have myself assisted in carrying out
the voluntary system at the London Lock Hospital for more
than twenty years, and for the last six years I have seen the
voluntary and compulsory systems at work side by side in
the same institution. From the exceptional opportunity
which I have thus had of witnessing them both, I am daily
more and more convinced that nothing but the compulsory
periodical examination of prostitutes, and their compulsory
detention in hospital till cured, will have any material
influence in diminishing the lamentable prevalence of venereal disease amongst the population. Voluntary lock hospitals may afford charitable relief to the individual sufferers,
but, from a sanitary point of view, I believe them to be
absolutely useless. From long experience of these women, I
know them to be, with rare exceptions, far too reckless of
consequences to apply for admission, and to seclude themselves for treatment, until their disease had reached a stage
which renders it impossible for them to pursue their calling
any longer, and until they have done all the mischief of
which they are capable. To treat them as *out-patients*, which
is now done on so large a scale at the various hospitals and
dispensaries, is a positive injury to the public health, by

* See page 40.

enabling them to practise prostitution with less pain to themselves, and for a longer period, than they would otherwise be enabled to do."

PERSONAL OBSERVATIONS OF THE WORKING OF THE ACTS IN ALDERSHOT, CHATHAM, PLYMOUTH, AND DEVONPORT.

Being anxious to see something of the practical working of the Acts, I availed myself of a favourable opportunity of doing so in September, 1875, and, by the permission of the Inspector of Certified Hospitals, I was enabled to visit those named. I have published in the *Medical Times and Gazette* the results of my observations, some of which I will repeat here.

The Hospitals.

I was greatly struck with one circumstance which presented itself very strongly in each hospital, viz., the number of empty beds. Formerly these hospitals, even with a gradually increased number of beds to their present total, were too small, and the most severe cases had to be selected and admitted. But the work done has for some time been telling, and venereal diseases are being gradually stamped out of all these districts. The following summary will show this. The first column shows the total number of beds, the second those occupied at the date of my visit:—

	Total.	Occupied.
London Female Lock Hospital (Government Side)	76	23
Aldershot	100	37
Chatham	68	23
Royal Albert Hospital, Devonport	162	44
Totals	406	127

This is a great encouragement to those who advocate extension of the Acts, as it removes one very formidable objection—that of expense. It is not necessary to erect large permanent lock hospitals ; a small one will suffice, with temporary wards at first for the large proportion of diseased prostitutes which will always be found in any unprotected district on the first introduction of the Acts. Another very remarkable circumstance, which at once arrested my attention, was that, with the exception of one or two at each hospital, all the patients were able to be up and about, suggesting that the great majority were suffering from very mild forms of disease, which proved on inquiry to be the case. I was informed that cases of secondary and tertiary syphilis are now comparatively rare ; gonorrhœa and simple sores comprise the greater proportion, with now and then a case of primary syphilis. The most scrupulous cleanliness and order prevailed in all the hospitals; the patients were most respectful in their demeanour, and, considering who they were and from whence they came, I could not help contrasting their appearance with the wretched creatures I have described in my last chapter as haunting the lower parts of this town, and (as I feel sure) to be found in all seaports. As I went through these hospitals I asked myself the question, " But for the greatly maligned Contagious Diseases Acts, where would these women be ? " Where, indeed ! For we might have waited long for voluntary efforts to provide even the hospital buildings and beds; while as to maintaining them in anything like pro- per efficiency, this would have been hopeless. And even had this been done, voluntary efforts could never have brought these women in soon enough, nor always induced them to stay long enough. If, therefore, these Acts had done nothing else except provide hospital accommodation in some- thing like proportion to its requirements, they are deserving of the greatest credit. But, as we shall see, they have done a great deal more.

In all the hospitals there is a chapel, which, without excessive adornment, is made to resemble a chapel, and is not, as is too often the case in hospitals, merely a room in which prayers are said. The efforts of the chaplain and matrons, in inducing inmates to abandon their present mode of life, and to return home to friends or enter a refuge, are attended with the greatest success ; and, though the duties of the medical officers are necessarily of a more strictly professional nature, their assistance in the work of reformation is of no small importance, and many an "unfortunate" owes her restoration to the paths of virtue to the kind words spoken in the examination-room.

The arrangements made for the periodical examination were most complete—calculated to insure the most perfect privacy, and with every regard to the feelings and comfort of the women.

The waiting-rooms at Aldershot, Chatham, Plymouth, and Devonport are large and thoroughly convenient; and the first object observed was a large notice, explaining fully how each woman might obtain her release from the examination by applying to the visiting surgeon, who, if satisfied by inquiry that she had abandoned prostitution, would direct that she should be relieved from further periodical examination. In the examining-room I found every arrangement for securing sufficient light; ample means for the perfect cleansing and disinfecting of instruments ; the couch on which the women are placed is made comfortable with cushions, while so arranged as to afford at once, and without difficulty, a perfectly satisfactory view of the genitals. The rule which permits no one to be present except the nurse is absolute ; and I was informed previously that I could not witness the examinations, at which, knowing the importance of this rule, I did not expect to be present.

PLYMOUTH, DEVONPORT, AND STONEHAVEN.

As Plymouth resembles Liverpool in being a seaport and
a great maritime highway, I was especially interested in
seeing the arrangements there, and acquiring full information. I was shown through the Royal Albert Hospital by
the resident surgeon, Mr. Thom ; Dr. Archer, R.N., the visiting surgeon under the Acts to this district, gave me every
information and assistance ; while Mr. Anniss, the inspector
of the special police, gave me full details of what had been
effected by him and his officers since the commencement of
the Acts in 1865. The following is a summary of what I
learned :—

When the Act of 1864 was first put into operation in
Plymouth and Devonport, in April, 1865, there were 356
brothels, and 1,770 prostitutes. The number of beds in the
Royal Albert Hospital, available for diseased females, was
38 ; and, as this was found wholly inadequate, increased
accommodation was provided as follows :—

February, 1866	...	...	Increased to 50.	
April,	″	...	″	62.
January, 1868	...	...	″	86.
February,	″	...	...	″	96.
March,	″	...	...	″	112.
April,	″			″	128.
May,	″	...	...	″	154.
July,	″	...	...	″	162.

It was not till this ample provision was afforded that any
effect was produced in reducing the amount of disease ; and,
though the Act of 1866 had been in force for two years, providing for the periodical examination of all known prostitutes, it was only when this large number of beds was available that all the prostitutes known to the police could be

registered and periodically examined. This circumstance will help to explain the following Table, and will serve to show how important it is, in giving or examining statistics, to be thoroughly conversant with all the circumstances. At the first glance, there would seem to be an increase of disease; but it will be seen that, after 1869, when the full effects of the increased accommodation had been felt, the numbers steadily diminished, with only one slight fluctuation for the year 1873.

ROYAL ALBERT HOSPITAL, DEVONPORT.

Total number of cases of venereal diseases admitted from 1865 to 1st October, 1875 :—

Year ending 30th Sept.,			Year ending 30th Sept.,		
1865		245.	1871	...	767.
1866	...	315.	1872	...	672.
1867	...	321.	1873	..	680.
1868	...	1081.	1874		534.
1869	...	1536.	1875	...	466.*
1870	...	935.			

The character of the disease had very materially changed. Formerly the patients showed the same neglect and want of ordinary cleanliness that we have to lament here; now the change is most marked, and those admitted show very mild forms of disease, principally gonorrhœa and simple sores. They attend the examinations with regularity, and there is a marked improvement in their demeanour and habits.

A very striking instance of the diminution of disease in the district since the Acts were first put into operation is shown in the following Tables.

* Compare these with returns on page 39. I regret to say that, in a former pamphlet, the returns for the years 1870 to 1875 were given incorrectly, which made them appear less favourable to the Acts. It is, however, an error on the right side.

Mr. Anniss shrewdly suspected that the returns of cases of venereal diseases admitted into the local workhouses would show whether the Acts had effected any reduction, and accordingly procured these from time to time. I have corresponded with the medical officers of these workhouses— Dr. Thomas, of Plymouth; Mr. De la Rue, of Devonport; and Mr. Leah, of Stonehouse; and they all assure me that the returns are perfectly correct, and attribute the marvellous result to the working of the Acts.

Return showing the number of paupers treated for venereal diseases in Plymouth, Devonport, and Stonehouse Workhouses, during the undermentioned periods of two years :—

Period of Two Years ending 30th Sept.	PLYMOUTH.			DEVONPORT.			STON'HOUSE.			Total.		Grand Total.
	Males.	Females.	Total.	Males.	Females.	Total.	Males.	Females.	Total.	Males.	Females.	
1864	53	239	292	32	91	123	...	56	56	85	386	471
1866	29	80	109	16	67	83	...	31	31	45	178	223
1868	27	54	81	6	44	50	...	33	33	33	131	164
1870	15	32	47	10	34	44	1	10	11	29	76	102
1872	13	2	15	5	2	7	...	...	...	18	4	22
*1874	6	3	9	1	2	3	...	...	...	7	5	12

Now, it might at first seem that the Royal Albert Hospital has simply taken the place of the workhouses; but a very little consideration will show that this cannot be the case. In the first place, males suffering from venereal disease are not admitted into the hospital, whilst their number in the above return has fallen from 85 to 7. Again, the large number admitted into hospital in 1868 and 1869 shows conclusively that many were admitted that would never have

* Compare these with Returns on pages 40 and 41.

applied to go into the workhouse. But the mild character of the cases admitted now is the strongest proof of all; such cases are scarcely ever seen in workhouses or voluntary lock hospitals. It is, therefore, impossible to escape from the conclusion that these diseases are being gradually stamped out of this district; and but for the importation of disease from Exeter, and other unprotected places, this would be even still more marked.

But the reduction of disease is by no means the only good which has been effected. The number of prostitutes in this district, which, as we have seen, was at first 1,770, has been reduced to about 400; the 356 brothels to 98. The state of the streets now presents a most remarkable contrast to what it was ten years ago. It was my first visit to Plymouth, hence I was unable to make any comparison; but I have been informed by professional and other friends, who remember Plymouth as it was in past years, and who describe its state then as very bad. It was impossible to walk the streets without being solicited, or even insulted by the lowest of women, whose language and demeanour were shocking. I could hardly believe that I was in a seaport when Mr. Anniss escorted me in the evening through the town. No crowds of drunken seamen and shameless women round public-houses were to be seen; and even those streets where brothels now exist were remarkably quiet and orderly. I observed the same state when I went by myself the next evening; and I feel sure that the freedom of the streets from the rampant solicitation which is to be seen in the lower parts of our great seaports must be attended with the happiest results, both to seamen and the inhabitants generally.

I regret to observe that Mr. Anniss has been singled out, in what I must term a most cowardly and unjustifiable manner, by a physician in this town, and other opponents of the Acts, who have subjected him to a series of most malignant attacks ; simply, as it would appear, because his work has been so well and efficiently performed. Such attacks will only recoil on those who make them ; and having had the advantage of seeing him, of examining his returns, observing the care with which they have been prepared, and the full explanations he is able to give of every detail, I am able to add my testimony to his worth. The authorities are to be congratulated on possessing so efficient and valuable an officer ; and I gladly avail myself of this opportunity of saying so. I may add that, in the district which is the sphere of his labours, Inspector Anniss is held in the highest esteem by all classes. For years I have had a pretty extensive acquaintance with police officers of all grades, and have often remarked what superior intelligence, tact, and dis-cretion is to be found amongst them. I could not imagine anyone more thoroughly competent to be intrusted with such difficult and delicate duties as the officer who has been subjected to such gross attacks.

The following extracts from the last report of the Com-mittee of the Royal Albert Hospital will be read with interest, showing, as it does, the excellent work done by the Acts in a moral and reformatory aspect :—

" 9. The difference between the number of beds occu-pied during the present year and the preceding one is mainly attributable to the diminution in the number of lock patients. This fact is so far satisfactory that it shows the beneficial operation of the Acts in force for the reduction of disease amongst that class. The committee continue to find that the results of the Acts, notwithstanding their want of many improvements, are successful, not only in a sanitary point of view, but, what is of far greater importance, in the promotion of morality and providing the means of reformation. The number of beds, on the original opening of the new wards, was 120, and these were not unfrequently full. In the past year, the average occupation has been 49·75, and at one period of the year the numbers had fallen to 33·53. No stronger evidence can be given as to the reduction of disease consequent upon the operations of these Acts. But it is also found that an increasing proportion of those who pass through the hospital are voluntarily accepting the offers which are before them for a return to a respectable and moral life.

"10. The committee refer with satisfaction to the following analysis of the quarterly and general reports of the chaplain :—

Total number included in the reports	80	
Not comprised in the above ...	9	
	—	
	89	
Deduct names twice entered ...	2	
	—	
	87	
Admitted to and still remaining in homes and penitentiaries	37	
Restored to friends, gone to service, and married, of whom good reports are received ...	40	
Relapsed	10	
	—	87."

RESULTS OF THE ACTS IN OTHER SEAPORTS.

The other places I visited — Chatham, Aldershot, and Windsor—showed results no less satisfactory than the above, though, as they are not seaports, I shall not give details. At Dartmouth (which is included in the Devonport district), out of eight women examined on the first introduction of the Acts, six were found seriously diseased, five with syphilis. This may seem to some a small matter ; but medical practitioners, who know how many men may be affected by one woman, will think differently. The number of prostitutes in Dartmouth has been reduced to two or three, and disease is almost unknown. At Sheerness, syphilis has been almost entirely eradicated from among the women of the town, this port possessing special advantages of situation. At Portsmouth, the reduction has been most considerable, though from its situation it is peculiarly liable to fresh importation of disease from unprotected stations.* At Southampton and Dover, the reduction of disease has been very great, though these ports are, like Portsmouth, peculiarly liable to importation.

The following extract of a letter from Dr. Gramshaw, the visiting surgeon under the Acts, and medical officer of health at Gravesend, which appeared in a recent number of the *British Medical Journal*, shows very clearly the excellent results in that town :—

" The tables of statistics put forward both by promoters and opponents of the Contagious Diseases Acts are frequently so bewildering to ordinary minds that they are cast aside without examination, and the statements of those who frame them are taken for granted, whatever may be the opinions they are wanted to produce.

" A statement of facts with regard to the working of the Acts amongst us in Gravesend, if unencumbered by tables, may perhaps be interesting to some, and may also be useful in the unsettled state of public opinion.

" We have on the books here a number of women, varying from thirty-five to forty, somewhat under half of whom are required to come up weekly for inspection. This, of course, represents the number of public prostitutes only. The behaviour of these women has been uniformly good.

---

* In the Portsea Union Workhouse, during the years 1870 to 1873 inclusive, there were only 13 males and 36 females admitted with venereal disease.

There has never been the slightest repugnance shown by any to examination. During my two years of office, I have known girls come into the district from Warley, and elsewhere, to present themselves for examination; but I never once heard or saw any unwillingness to submit to it on the score of modesty from a single patient. A few object to the trouble it gives them, of getting clean clothes and of regularity of hours, but never from any other cause. No officer here has ever been found overstepping the limits of his duty. In the last four months I have been obliged to send only one woman to hospital for decided disease, and either three or four others as doubtful cases, whose detention has only been for a short period.

"In private practice here I rarely see a case of syphilis, either in men or women, certainly not contracted in the town. In conversation with other medical men, I hear their experience is nearly the same. At all events, the amount in the last few years is very much lessened. The chemists, who used themselves to treat a great many venereal diseases, make a similar statement.

"Our barracks contain a variable number of soldiers. I believe the average to be about 400. Since June 17th, in last year, there have been in the Military Hospital no more than three cases of disease; one only of these is ascribed to Gravesend; the other two were contracted before the men came here. When we take this last statement into consideration, and recollect that, though not exactly a port, vessels are always passing and repassing on the river, and that they are often detained here for a day or two, we may fairly give credit to the Acts, and to their repressive and protective powers, for much of this freedom from a horrible scourge.

"To those who would accuse us, as they often do, of bringing up for examination women who are only suspected of prostitution, we reply that nothing of the sort ever takes place. It is necessary to be certain of their character before they are summoned to attend ; and, though there are now and then cases where the suspicion is very strong, yet the Acts are never put in force against them till certainty exists. To such as publicly commit themselves, we say, ' We are powerless to prevent you exercising your calling, if you will persist in doing so ; but we can, and will, to a certain extent, prevent your becoming the source of irreparable mischief to infants and unoffending victims.' All this takes place quietly and decorously, in a secluded part of the town, and the next-door neighbours cannot, and do not, complain of it as offensive. If any part of the system can possibly be called objectionable, it is well counterbalanced by results. How much better the state of things at present than some years ago, when nothing prohibitory was in force ! Surely, opposition arises from ignorance, and from ignorance only."

The Extension of the Acts to Liverpool.

Liverpool is undoubtedly larger than any town or district to which the Acts have been hitherto applied ; hence a fear on the part of many, who are not unfavourable to their extension here, that the large area, and consequently large expense, would be insuperable objections. I have been assured by those who have assisted in the administration of the Acts, in large and small districts, that there is no more difficulty in dealing with a large than with a small one. And, in his evidence before the Lords' committee, Captain Harris, Assistant Commissioner of Metropolitan Police, expressed a strong opinion that the extension of the Acts to the metropolis was perfectly feasible.

As Liverpool is neither a garrison town nor naval seaport, the administration would probably have to be under a different Government department; and, seeing the large proportion of merchant seamen here, we might naturally look to the Board of Trade as the proper one to be intrusted with all those duties which, in places, under the Acts, are undertaken by the War Office or Admiralty.

Moreover, it would be unnecessary to employ metropolitan police, as we have in Liverpool a most efficient police force, with many most superior and intelligent officers, from whom might be selected a sufficient number, perfectly competent to be intrusted with this special service.

The first step would be to ascertain the exact number of common prostitutes, which could not be a matter of great difficulty, since it has been done annually for many years. It would, however, be much more accurately performed by special police, whose duties were confined to this service, and who verified their returns by going over the ground repeatedly. Again, the present returns are taken in September, when, for many reasons, the number of prostitutes is probably less than at other times of the year. This preliminary to the "cleansing of the Augean stable' would be attended with marvellous results here, as it has been elsewhere. Many a den of abomination which has been permitted to exist year after year would, from the daylight thus introduced, be swept away. Many a street that is now entirely composed of the abodes of filthy and diseased prostitutes would, after a few visits of the special police, assume a totally different appearance to what it now presents.

Hospital Accommodation.

When the whole number of common prostitutes was ascertained, we should be in a better position to judge as to what number of beds would be required for those found to be diseased. But without waiting for this, it may at once be assumed that a large temporary accommodation would be required, though a permanent hospital accommodation of seventy or eighty beds would probably be sufficient. We have seen that 162 beds were required at Devonport; at Portsmouth, 120 were at first not at all too many; at Aldershot, 100; while subsequently, in all of these, little more than a third of the beds were required. Hence, by adopting a small hospital with large temporary accommodation, a considerable expenditure may be saved. The new wing of the London Lock Hospital was erected at an expense of not quite £80 per bed, including every expense necessary for occupation. Thus, a hospital with fifty beds could be erected for £4,000, while adjoining temporary wooden hospitals could be constructed at an expense of £20 per bed. I believe that with compulsory powers, judicious management, and careful selection of cases, we could, with an accommodation of two hundred and fifty or three hundred beds, reduce in a few months the amount of disease among the prostitutes of this town to the same ratio as is seen elsewhere; that is, instead of being at least forty per cent., it might be reduced to half or even less.

Expense of Hospital Management.

I find that the annual cost of the London Lock Hospital is £24 10s. per bed, supposing each bed to be constantly filled. Our Lock Hospital here costs less than £20 per bed, but, as we have seen, each bed is not constantly filled; were it so, I believe the cost would just equal the above amount of £24 10s. The cost of three hundred beds constantly occupied would be, for six months, £3,675; for three months, £1,837 10s. An outlay of £10,000 for hospitals, and an additional sum of £5,000, would probably cover the whole expense of the first year's administration of the Acts here; while if accommodation could be procured in other hospitals this might be considerably reduced. The second year's expenses would probably not be half this amount, which would decrease with each successive year. Surely, for the first seaport in the kingdom, this is not a very great charge, especially when the enormous benefits which would undoubtedly arise are borne in mind.

THE STATE OF OTHER SEAPORTS NOT UNDER THE ACTS AS REGARDS PROSTITUTION AND DISEASE.

Much of what I have said as regards Liverpool will apply to other seaports where large numbers of merchant seamen are to be found. From the Returns, No. 1 and 3, in the Appendix, it will be seen that, with one or two exceptions, the Lock Hospital accommodation is most inadequate in all the towns I have given. Though my object is more specially to deal with seaports, I have given inland towns and cities to show that this want of lock hospital accommodation is general; and from the dates it will be observed that, with the exception of Bristol, no voluntary lock hospital has been established since the agitation arose in connection with these Acts. From inquiries I have made, and other sources of information, I am enabled to give the following brief details as to five seaports :—

BRISTOL.—The population of this port was, at the last census, 182,522. I have been unable to obtain any reliable return of the number of brothels and prostitutes known to the police, but it is well known that in some parts of Bristol both are to be found in large numbers; and from the description given me, by a medical friend, of the lower parts of the town, I should judge that their condition is not much better than the state of similar localities in this town. A lock hospital with sixteen beds, which can be increased to twenty, was, in 1870, established by the exertions of Mr. R. W. Coe, Consulting-Surgeon to the Bristol General Hospital, who has been enabled to keep it on by the assistance of friends. It is only fair, however, that I should state that Mr. Coe is not in favour of any extension of these Acts, and believes that if lock hospitals were more general, and well conducted, a large influence would be exercised over the physical maladies, and a larger one over the moral ones. In writing to him, I have expressed a fear that he will be greatly disappointed with the result of voluntary efforts to deal with this evil, and I may here remark that if 162 beds were required at Devonport (which, combined with Plymouth, is much less populous than Bristol), the results obtained by 16 beds, even if kept constantly filled, will be hardly felt. This is quite independent of the other disadvantages of the voluntary system as compared with the compulsory. Only very exceptional cases of venereal disease in either sex are admitted into the two hospitals of Bristol, though among the out-patients at either hospital a large number are, I believe, seen.

Bristol Union Workhouse.

Number of paupers treated for venereal disease in the lock wards, in the years 1871 to 1875, both inclusive :—

NUMBERS OF PATIENTS.

Year.		Male.		Female.		Total.
1871	...	112	...	74		186
1872	...	101		86	...	187
1873		112	...	84	...	196
1874	...	118	...	101	...	219
1875	...	100	...	80	...	180

Dr. Henry Grace, the medical officer of this workhouse, to whose kindness I am indebted for the above, states :—"Many others, with secondary and tertiary symptoms, are about the house in a chronic and less virulent form, principally amongst the middle-aged and aged, and many infants' (congenital) cases that are not treated in lock wards. Thus I cannot furnish you with the accurate number." It will be observed that here the number of males exceeds that of females.

CARDIFF.—The population of this seaport was, according to the last census, 56,911. From the Chief Constable I have received a letter, which gives the information I required so clearly, and is in other respects so important, that I give it *in extenso* :—

"Many thanks for the interesting pamphlet you have sent me. There is no question in the minds of those whose duties bring them in contact with the prostitution of towns of the practical, invaluable good resulting from the Contagious Diseases Acts of 1866 and 1869; and the immense benefit derived from them, socially and morally, is proved from facts from which there is no escape. It is unfortunate that *sentiment* should be such a stumbling-block to their extension universally throughout the kingdom; however, half a loaf is better than no bread, and if our seaport towns could be brought under their influence, it would be a step in the right direction, and would tend more to the moral regeneration of the people than the present futile efforts of religious bodies. Here, in Cardiff, we have a patent fact of the inability of religion *per se* to cope with the evil of prostitution, which is rampant in the lower parts of the town, and amongst whom order is only maintained by the supervision of the police.

"We have in Cardiff about eighty brothels, containing on an average two hundred women, known to the police. As we are a seaport, with large docks, your remarks, and those of Major Greig, apply word for word to Cardiff, and I can add my testimony to the utterly abominable lives led by women who have given themselves over to prostitution.

"I was a district superintendent of police for many years in India, where the Acts, or similar ones, are carried out in every cantonment with the most marvellous results, and concerning their practical benefit, in both lessening disease and increasing morality, there is but one universally expressed opinion of praise. You are at liberty to make any use of my opinion."

No cases of venereal disease are admitted into the Cardiff, Glamorganshire, and Monmouthshire Infirmary, which is the only hospital here. Dr. Sheen, medical officer to the Cardiff Workhouse, has kindly sent me the returns for the last three years of patients admitted with venereal diseases :—

Year.	Females.	Males.	
1873 ...	93 ...	19	of whom 8 were sailors.
1874 ...	73 ...	28	″ 11 ″
1875. ...	57 ...	38	″ 15 ″

Dr. Sheen accounts for the decrease in females as possibly due to the compulsory detention which is here enforced. Be this as it may, I think the figures, taken in conjunction with the Chief Constable's description of the two hundred prostitutes, suggest a very terrible state of matters in this seaport. I am very glad to be able to state that, among the medical profession in Cardiff, there is an almost unanimous feeling in favour of the Acts, and of their extension to that port.

DUBLIN.—Population at the last census, 246,326. I have not any statistics of prostitution, but it is well known that venereal diseases are very prevalent here ; and this is more to be regretted, as it will be observed that the hospital accommodation for such diseases is more ample than in any town or city not protected by the Acts. There are 60 beds in the Westmoreland Lock Hospital, always ready and generally full, and Mr. T. D. Rice, the Resident Apothecary, informs me that the number of patients hardly ever gets below 50. There is house-room for 150 beds, and with periodical examinations of all known prostitutes, compulsory admission and detention in hospital, and a full use of the ample hospital accommodation provided, I feel sure that

Dublin might soon be as free from venereal diseases as the neighbouring camp of The Curragh, or the City of Cork. The Westmoreland Lock Hospital receives a grant from Government, and it is instructive to see the difference here between voluntary and compulsory efforts. The Kildare Hospital has 40 beds, that at Cork 46, which are more than sufficient, and the districts in which they are situated are comparatively free from disease. On the other hand, Dublin is a hotbed of disease, though the voluntary hospital accommodation is more than double that of Cork or The Curragh.

GLASOW.—Population at the last census, 490,442. From the criminal returns of the city police, kindly forwarded me by the Chief Constable, Mr. A. McCall, I find that in 1875 the number of prostitutes apprehended for importuning passengers upon the streets for the purpose of prostitution, was 1,889, against 1,430 the preceding year, and for harbouring prostitutes and managing brothels, 41 persons were brought before the courts. According to a Table (No. 11) in this return, there were known to the police 40 brothels and 57 prostitutes, showing a considerable reduction from former years, as in 1870 the brothels numbered 204, and the prostitutes living in them 559.

To the Superintendent of the Glasgow Lock Hospital for Females I am indebted for the reports of that hospital for the years 1870 to 1875, both inclusive, from which I extract the following :—

NUMBER OF PATIENTS.

Year.			Admitted.
1870			534
1871			394
1872	...	...	369
1873			405
1874	...	..	436
1875	...	. .	...	402

In their report for last year the medical officers state that
"from careful observations of the character of the disease, as
it has presented itself to the medical officers, the conclusion
has been arrived at that of late years its virulence has been
pretty much diminished; and this they consider may be
owing to the fact that patients suffering from disease find
ready access to the institution, the doors of which are always
open to those who need its aid." This is very satisfactory,
but if compulsory powers were available, with the resources
of this hospital (60 to 70 beds), the prevalence of the disease
might soon be reduced. The above numbers, it will be seen,
fluctuate, but do not diminish.

HULL.—Population at the last census, 123,408. I have
received from the Chief Constable, Mr. Cook, the criminal
returns of the Hull police for last year, from which I extract
the details given on the following page.

There is no lock hospital in Hull, and I have been
informed that there was at first some opposition to the
admission of venereal cases into the Hull General Infirmary
on the part of some of the governors. The cases admitted
are, however, not many, but a large number are treated as
out-patients. Hull has figured rather prominently and
unenviably in some of the reports of the medical officers
of the navy who have had charge of ships in this
port. Thus, the surgeon of Her Majesty's ship *Auda-
cious*, writing, in 1870, in his annual report of the health of
the crew for the year 1872, describes the lower parts of the
town as a "*filthy focus of foul prostitutes, reckless and
degraded seamen.*" During the year, in an average force of
416 men, there were 125 cases of syphilis, being an annual
ratio of 300 per 1,000. Again, the contrast between the
ratio of disease in the coastguard ships at Hull and Southampton, respectively, during the same six years, 1868 to

RETURN OF THE NUMBER OF BROTHELS AND PROSTITUTES IN THE BOROUGH OF KINGSTON-UPON-HULL.

CLASSIFICATION OF THE HOUSES.	Number of Houses in which Prostitutes are kept.	Number of Houses of Accommodation to which Prostitutes resort.	Number of Prostitutes in the Borough of Kingston-upon-Hull.	Ages of Prostitutes.			
				15 and under 20 years	20 and under 25 years	25 and under 30 years	Above 30 years.
HOUSES IN WHICH PROSTITUTES ARE KEPT.							
First Class—Well conducted, the Girls not being Street Walkers	22	...	34	6	10	11	7
Second Class—Well conducted, and frequented by the Middle Classes and Youths	11	...	19	2	7	4	6
Third Class—Disorderly Houses, and frequented by the Lower Orders	103	...	407	33	157	105	112
HOUSES OF ACCOMMODATION TO WHICH PROSTITUTES RESORT.							
First Class—Well conducted, the Girls not being Street Walkers	...	6	...	...	...	...	...
Second Class—Well conducted, and frequented by the Middle Classes and Youths	...	7	...	...	...	...	...
Third Class—Disorderly Houses, and frequented by the Lower Orders	...	10	...	...	...	...	...
Number of known Prostitutes who resort to Houses of Accommodation, but not to any House in particular	...	...	138	19	36	39	44
TOTAL	226	23	598	60	210	159	169

1873, is very striking. The Acts were first enforced at Portsmouth in 1869, and at Southampton in 1870. The following is the result : —

Hull.		Southampton.	
Year.	Ratio of disease.	Year.	Ratio of disease.
1868	... 111 per 1,000.	1868	... 104 per 1,000.
1871	... 155 „ .	1869	... 69 „
1873	... 100 „	1870	... 37 „
		1873	... 26 „

Mean ratio for the last four years, 124 per 1,000.

Mean ratio for the last four years, 31 per 1,000.

THE OPPONENTS OF THE ACTS IN LIVERPOOL.

Liverpool is well known as a stronghold for the opponents of the Acts, and it is not to be expected that such measures should not excite opposition. I must point out, however, that the Acts had been in force for some years, and it was not till their extension was actually proposed to Liverpool that we heard of any opposition. I should have been very glad to have been able to give the excellent ladies and gentlemen who oppose these Acts credit for having done so in a very practical way, by spending their time, money, and other resources in one or both of the following ways :—

(1.) By assisting the committee of the Royal Infirmary to increase the accommodation in the Lock Hospital, so as to enable them to classify the female patients, and contributing towards the increased annual expenditure.

(2.) By organising some means by which prostitutes might be induced to enter the hospital as soon as diseased, and by aiding others in promoting their reform.

Instead of this, I regret to say that large quantities of the "horrible literature," so eloquently denounced by Mr.

Hardy, have emanated from Liverpool; and quite recently married ladies with families living here have been told that if ever the Contagious Diseases Acts were brought to Liverpool, their daughters would not be able to walk the streets safely; an infamous falsehood which cannot be too strongly and emphatically contradicted. I myself saw in the streets of the royal borough of Windsor, the ancient cathedral city of Canterbury, in Chatham, Plymouth and Devonport, ladies and women of all ages walking in the streets in perfect safety, many of whom, I am happy to think, are not even aware that such Acts are in force, even in spite of the "horrible literature." The well-meaning but mistaken people who oppose the Acts have turned their backs on Liverpool, forgetting that charity begins at home, and spent their talents in places where there was no need of their efforts. It is sad, indeed, to think of the unhappy women and girls I have described as to be found in the lower parts of this town being left in their filth and degradation, whilst those who might here have found a noble work, have left it to oppose elsewhere the first and only real attempts that have ever been made to cope with the "social evil."

In consequence of mis-statements made at public meetings in Bradford and this town, about the end of 1874, the following memorial was drawn up for presentation to the Home Secretary :—

To the Right Honourable R. A. Cross, Her Majesty's Secretary of State for the Home Department.

"It having been publicly stated that of the Medical Practitioners in Liverpool not more than twenty-six could be induced to sign a memorial in favour of the Contagious Diseases Acts, and that at the present time it would be impossible to find twelve medical men in Liverpool who are favourable to the said Acts: We, the undersigned Medical Practitioners of Liverpool, beg to express our approval of the Acts as at present in operation in seventeen Garrison Towns and Ports in the United Kingdom, and to state that we are not in favour of a repeal of those Acts."

I undertook to procuro signatures, and in the course of a few days obtained upwards of eighty, including, with very few exceptions, all the leading physicians and surgeons in this town, and subsequently, by means of a circular, these were increased to more than one hundred and .seventy. As a specimen of the tactics of the opponents, I may give Mr. Stansfeld's remarks on this memorial, at a public meeting in this town, as reported in a local paper :—

" They had heard something in Liverpool lately of a medical memorial which had been addressed to the Home Secretary, and he marked something in that memorial of a hundred and sixty or a hundred and seventy Liverpool doctors to which he would ask attention. The memorial did not say that they approved of the principles of the Acts ; it did not ask that the Acts should be extended to the civil population ; in fact, the memorial was a remarkably worded document, negative in its character. The memorialists wished it to be understood that they were not in favour of the repeal of the Acts, which applied to seventeen districts of the country where military and naval quarters were to be found. If the medical profession assumed to speak with weight when addressing the Secretary of State or the legislature on a question of that kind, they ought to speak with frankness. He would ask those medical men, Were they in favour of the extension of the Acts to the whole country or not ? Because, if the medical argument was of any value at all, it was an argument in favour of the universal application of the Acts. Was or was it not the medical argument that the diseases consequent on the vices of men were so great a scourge that in the interests of innocence and future generations it was necessary to stamp them out ? If it was, what did they mean by simply telling the Secretary of State that they were not in favour of the repeal of the Acts, applying the law simply to the seventeen districts where soldiers and sailors were assembled ? If their opinion was that the diseases were a scourge which they ought all to endeavour to stamp out by certain exceptional hygienic conditions and laws, let them have the courage to state that opinion to Parliament or the Government."

I think that the right honourable gentleman's warmest admirers must admit that the above speech shows him to be most lamentably deficient in that very quality of frankness which he appears so anxious to inculcate on others. The object of the memorial was simply to correct a little mistake which had been made by others, and repeated by Mr. Stansfeld himself, only two months prior to his having to unsay it. A more wilful determination to evade a plain issue, or more deliberate instance of choosing to misunderstand what I maintain was a perfectly " frank " statement, I have never read. When the medical practitioners who signed the foregoing memorial are agreed that the Acts ought to be extended, I will undertake to say that they " will have the courage to state that opinion to Parliament or the Government." And I will also undertake to say that when they have so stated it, they will not disown their own words, as Mr. Stansfeld did, when his own words were quoted,—" Acts which are passed without the sanction of public opinion, and without that preliminary discussion which the laws of Parliament are intended to receive, have no rightful claim upon our obedience."

SUGGESTIONS.

Those I have to make may be divided into two classes : (1) Those which refer to such further voluntary efforts as may be made to diminish the fearful evils of prostitution and disease in seaports ; (2) Those which belong to future legislation, (*a.*) SAILORS' HOMES.—I would suggest that attached to all these useful institutions there should be dispensaries for the special treatment of venereal diseases, on the self-supporting principle. A payment of one shilling for each attendance for all seamen, with graduated fees for petty and other officers, would pay all expenses, and leave a balance for an *honorarium* for the medical officer. Such an arrangement would bring these cases as early as possible under treatment, and do more to exterminate the quack fraternity than any legal prosecutions.

(*b.*) HOSPITAL ACCOMMODATION FOR MALES. ·—Though it seems very hopeless, I would suggest that increased hospital accommodation on the voluntary system, for those men whose cases are too severe for dispensary treatment, might be provided. If shipowners were, as they ought to be, more strongly represented on the managing committee of the hospitals and infirmaries in our seaports, I think this defect would be remedied. A small ward, isolated from the rest of the hospital, containing from six to ten beds, with separate water-closets, a male nurse, and other requirements, would be a very little extra charge on a general hospital, and the benefits would be incalculable. I may here cite on this subject so high an authority as Mr. Prescott Hewett, Consulting Surgeon to St. George's Hospital, who, in his evidence before the Lords' Committee, says, " It would be to the interest of every hospital that there should be a syphilitic ward in it, and I have no doubt in my own mind that the thing must come to that by-and-by. It is to the interest of all our hospitals to teach in our schools, and we must teach everything, and, as a matter of teaching, unless we have the patients to teach from we cannot teach ; and I have no doubt that in the course of time, if there were a little pressure put upon the hospitals, every hospital would be too glad to do it." Mr. Hewett must regret to see that, instead of such being the case, the beds set apart in St. Bartholomew's and Guy's Hospitals for venereal diseases have been reduced in number, while those in King's College and the Royal Free Hospitals have been closed to such cases altogether. When it is borne in mind how difficult it is to raise and maintain institutions for the most worthy and deserving objects, orphan children, the blind, deaf-mutes, etc., it will be readily conceived how difficult it is to provide lock hospitals. And though the providing of lock wards in general hospitals would appear to be an easy matter, it will be found that, practically, such is not the case, and that very strong pressure must be brought to bear on the managers of hospitals if these wards are to become general, and form an essential part of every hospital and infirmary.

(c.) FEMALE LOCK HOSPITALS.—The experience of our Lock Hospital here so thoroughly confirms all that Mr. Lane has said,* that I have no hope of our ever being able to effect any permanent reduction of disease among common prostitutes by means of these voluntary hospitals. However well conducted they may be, women will not enter them till they are suffering to such an extent that they cannot continue prostitution any longer. At this date (June 20th) there are only six beds occupied on the female side of our hospital out of a total of twenty-five, though, as we have seen, there are in all probability hundreds of diseased women about the streets. Much ignorance prevails amongst them, and I have too much reason to fear that, though our hospital has existed for more than forty years, many of them are not aware of its existence. And, though it will be scarcely credited, there still remains a superstitious belief, both among men and women, that incurable cases in lock hospitals

* See pages 16 and 47.

are disposed of by smothering! If some organisation could
be arranged by which brothels and their inmates could be
visited, information furnished as to lock hospitals, and the
minds of those willing to go to them disabused of the absurd
superstition alluded to, then the full benefit of these institutions might be utilised. But so much difficulty surrounds
any such voluntary organisation, that I can do no more than
name it.

(d.) REFUGES, HOMES FOR FALLEN WOMEN,
PENITENTIARIES, Etc.—There are, I am glad to say, five
of these most excellent charities in and near Liverpool, and I
willingly take this opportunity of saying how much the unfortunate inmates, as well as the public generally, are indebted
to those who founded and maintain them. The sugges-
tions I would make to those who conduct these charities is,
that they should avoid as much as possible giving the inmates
menial labour, such as washing and mangling, remembering
from what a life they have come, in which work of any kind
is scrupulously avoided. They will be found deplorably
deficient in the knowledge of needlework, which is not
menial, and may be of great advantage to them. Again,
many of them have good voices and a talent for music, and
this they may cultivate with great advantage. Of the 172
females who entered our hospital last year, no fewer than 32
were sent home to their friends, to the Benevolent Home,
Penitentiary, or Reformatory. It is rather a common practice with the opponents of the Acts to throw doubt and discredit on their reformatory work. But if by voluntary efforts,
acting on a small number, we can achieve such a result as
the above, what might not be done had we double the number
of beds constantly filled? It is simply a question of numbers; out of the larger number will be the larger proportion
of reformations.

(e.) SELECT COMMITTEE OF INQUIRY INTO THE PREVALENCE AND SEVERITY OF VENEREAL DISEASES AT MERCANTILE SEAPORTS.—If I have proved my case, I hope that the shipowners of this and the other seaports I have named will be induced to petition the Board of Trade for a committee of inquiry similar to what was made in 1862 with respect to the army and navy. There could not be a more favourable time than the present, as we are promised that the subject of the health of the mercantile marine is to receive the attention of the House of Commons next session. Considering the large number of merchant vessels employed in the postal and other Government service, it seems to me that this is especially a subject for a Government inquiry. The last paragraph of the Report of the Venereal Committee of 1864 may be given as confirming this :—

"The committee confidently believe that if the foregoing recommendations were acted upon with energy, the amount of venereal disease might be greatly reduced amongst the men of the army and navy. They cannot ignore, however, the existence of a fertile source of disease in the seaport towns which the Contagious Diseases Prevention Act, even as proposed to be amended, would still leave untouched, viz., that which is introduced by the sailors of the merchant service of our own and other nations. These men, it is well known, are frequently diseased, and often remain for a long period without any kind of treatment. This involves so many important considerations that the committee only venture to call serious attention to the subject."

The subject has frequently been noticed since, and I may here repeat the words of the Royal Commissioners :—

"But we think that, for the public good, particular districts which are, from any cause, peculiarly liable to contagious disease, should be subjected to special sanitary regulations. We therefore approve of the establishment of hospitals at the public charge, and of police regulations enforced under central authority within such districts."

What places can be more peculiarly liable to contagious diseases than our seaports, where large numbers of seamen are besieged on their landing by diseased prostitutes, and where the hospital accommodation for such diseases may be said, with one or two exceptions, to be almost *nil*?

(*f.*) COMPULSORY MEDICAL EXAMINATION OF ALL MERCHANT SEAMEN ON ARRIVAL AND DEPARTURE.—Though, in the Merchant Shipping Act of 1851, a clause was inserted providing for the medical examination of merchant seamen before sailing, it has practically been of no effect, as it was voluntary and not compulsory. It has been repeatedly urged, and with great reason, that it should be made compulsory. Nothing can be more unfair to shipowners than for a seaman to proceed to sea as thoroughly competent to fulfil the duties he has undertaken, or, in nautical phraseology, to "ship as able seaman," when at that very moment, or within a few days after, he may be suffering from a disease that renders him thoroughly unfit to perform many of the duties he has agreed to perform under the ship's articles. It is an unfair bargain, of which shipowners may justly complain; and though the men may conceal their complaints, and do their duties more or less, the mischief does not end there. What can be more reasonable than for shipowners to require of every man, before he signs articles, a certificate that he is free from any disease or disorder which may incapacitate him for duty on board ship? The expense would be trifling, and all which, I feel sure, would be willingly borne.

Again, on the arrival of a vessel at port, a modification of the above might be adopted. It could be easily ascertained whether any of the crew were suffering from a contagious disorder, and such should be sent to hospital. The only difficulty would be, as we have seen, the want of sufficient hospital accommodation.

(f.) Should the committee of inquiry be appointed, and their report confirm what I have here stated, one only result can follow, viz., a recommendation that the Acts should be extended to such seaports as are the objects of inquiry, either in their present or in some amended form. And looking at all the facts; seeing the results at Plymouth, Devonport, Sheerness, Gravesend, Dartmouth, etc., such an extension can, if carried out with proper care, only be attended with the happiest results, medically, morally, and socially.

Conclusion.

I have now answered the very uninviting but important questions with which I commenced this Paper. I have shown that in this town venereal diseases have not diminished in frequency nor severity, and that the same remark applies to Bristol, Cardiff, Dublin, Glasgow, and Hull, with some modifications in the case of Glasgow. I have shown, on the other hand, that in certain other seaports these diseases have considerably diminished in frequency, whilst their type has assumed a much milder form. I have also shown that, at the same time, the moral and social improvement of these latter has been at least on a par with the physical. From my own observations, I could not imagine, on the one hand, anything more disastrous to those places than would be the repeal of these much-abused Acts, which have achieved such wonderful results; nor, on the other hand, could I imagine anything more beneficial than would be their extension, if not generally, at least to those places where the evils they have so much mitigated elsewhere are still rampant. The matter will, in all probability, again engage the attention of Parliament shortly after this is published, when I trust that something more will be done than merely rejecting the motion for the repeal of these Acts.

I would here notice, very briefly, two objections which are generally raised, and which, having more special regard to the medical question, I have left unnoticed. It is urged that, by removing the fear of contracting disease, we incur the risk of promoting immorality and vice. This objection has been a favourite one with many clergy, and others, who regard it as altogether unanswerable, and shelter themselves behind it as their impregnable strong point. It is, unfortunately for them, founded on false premises, and therefore the deductions must also be false. It has its origin in ignorance, for if it be true, the converse must be true, that men and women who have once contracted the disease are deterred from immoral conduct in future. The experience of hospital and private practice completely dispels such an idea; the same men and women come to the lock hospital again and again; in private practice, the same patient presents himself for the sixth, tenth, or twelfth attack of this disease. But more than this. What do those who use such an argument say in effect? They say this, " We are very sorry to be compelled to state that our efforts to teach chastity and purity are vain. We cannot persuade men and women to be pure and chaste because it is their duty to be so; we must hold out *in terrorem* the fear of a foul and loathsome disease; take that fear away, and we are helpless." I am glad to see that many clergy are alive to the very false position in which they must be placed by clinging to this objection. Let them do their part, and leave the medical part of the question to those who are competent to deal with it.

The other objection is, that the Acts virtually recognise

prostitution. Now, I have given Tables of brothels and prostitutes in this and other towns; I have shown that in Hull the former are divided into three classes, the third class comprising " Disorderly houses frequented by the lower orders"; that in Cardiff 80 brothels, with 200 prostitutes, are known to the police, the chief constable describing as " thoroughly abominable" the lives led by the women who have given themselves over to prostitution. I have also shown that, in Liverpool, proceedings are taken in most cases where young girls are kept or robberies committed; where they are of notoriously bad character, and have become a public nuisance; where they are opened in a respectable street or leading thoroughfare, and where they are complained of by two or more of the inhabitants of the street, who were prepared to substantiate their complaints in court; but that, in spite of all this, the Table shows 420 brothels. As it is an indictable offence to keep a brothel under any circumstances whatever, it must be admitted that brothels and prostitutes are, and have long been, recognised. The principle of recognition has thus already been fully conceded, and to raise it as an objection to the Acts is childish trifling with a serious subject. It is only by placing them under the supervision of a special police that the fearful evils prevalent can be dealt with; and I conclude with the words of a well-known French author, Parent Duchâtelet, which express better than any words I could use what legislation may do : —

" If legislation cannot render men virtuous; if it cannot correct the judgment, and repress the impetuosity of passions which appeal to their senses too loudly to leave them the consciousness of duty; at least it may meet the danger to which the imprudent expose themselves, and, for the sake of these men's wives and children, look after the health of the guilty in order to preserve the innocent. I will go further, for I maintain that it ought to do so, and that those who have neglected this important duty have been unfaithful to their trust, and can only be excused by their ignorance of the benefits of the sanitary surveillance of prostitution."

APPENDIX. No. 1.

Return showing all the Lock Hospitals (both Government and Voluntary) in the United Kingdom.

County.	Town or City.	Year when first opened.	Number of Beds.		
			Male.	Female.	Total.
Bedfordshire - - ⎫					
Berkshire - - ⎪					
Buckinghamshire - ⎪	No Lock Hospital				
Cambridgeshire - ⎬	in any of these				
Cheshire - - ⎪	Counties.				
Cornwall - - ⎪					
Cumberland - - ⎪					
Derbyshire - - ⎭					
Devonshire - -	Devonport (V.G.)-	1863	None.	100	100*
Dorsetshire - - ⎫	None in either				
Durham - - ⎭	County.				
Essex - - -	Colchester (G.) -		None.	25	25
Gloucestershire -	Bristol (V.) -	1870	None.	16	16
Hampshire - -	Aldershot (G.) -	1865	None.	100	100
Ditto - - ⎰	Portsmouth (V.G.) (Royal Portsmouth, Portsea, and Gosport Hospital) - -	1851	None.	100	100†
Herefordshire - ⎫	None in any of				
Hertfordshire - ⎬	these Counties.				
Huntingdonshire - ⎭					
Kent - - -	Chatham (G.) -	1870	None.	62	62
Ditto - - -	Shorncliffe (G.) -	1868	None.	25	25
Lancashire - -	Liverpool (V.) -	1834	25	25	50
Ditto -	Manchester (V.) -	1819	None.	50	50
Leicestershire - ⎫	None in either.				
Lincolnshire - ⎭					
Middlesex - -	London (V.G.) -	1746	20	166	186
Monmouthshire - ⎫					
Norfolk - - ⎪					
Northamptonshire- ⎪					
Northumberland - ⎪					
Nottinghamshire - ⎪					
Oxfordshire - - ⎪					
Rutlanshire - - ⎪					
Shropshire - - ⎬	None in any of				
Somersetshire - ⎪	these Counties.				
Staffordshire- - ⎪					
Suffolk - - - ⎪					
Surrey - - - ⎪					
Sussex - - - ⎪					
Warwickshire - ⎪					
Wiltshire - - ⎪					
Worcestershire - ⎪					
Yorkshire - - ⎭					

Those marked (G) are entirely Government Hospitals. Those marked (V.G.) partly Government and partly Voluntary. Those marked (V.) are entirely Voluntary.
* Can be increased to 162.   † Can be increased to 120.

APPENDIX. No. 1.—*Continued.*

WALES.

There is no Lock Hospital in Wales.

SCOTLAND.

The only Lock Hospital is that of Glasgow, which has accommodation for between 60 and 70 patients. Only females are admitted, and Dr. Dunlop has informed me that the Hospital has usually half its beds unoccupied.

IRELAND.

There are Lock Hospitals in:—

Cork - with	46	Beds.	
Kildare - „	40	„	
Dublin, Westmoreland Lock Hospital, with	150	„	All for females.
	236	**Beds.**	

The Hospitals in Cork and Kildare are Government Hospitals for patients admitted under the Acts. The Westmoreland Lock Hospital is partly supported by Government, but is, as regards the admission of patients, a Voluntary Hospital. In it 60 beds are always ready, and 150 could be provided.

APPENDIX. No. 2.

Return showing the accommodation appropriated to Venereal In-patients at the various Hospitals of London.

Name of Hospital.	Beds. Male.	Beds. Female.	Remarks.
Charing Cross -	None.	None.	
King's College -	None.	None.	There was formerly a ward for females, with 6 beds; now abolished.
Royal Free - -	None.	None.	Formerly had 26 beds for females.
St. Mary's - -	None.	None.	
St. George's - -			No special beds, but cases admitted.
The London - -			„ „ „
University College -			„ „ „
The Lock (Special)-	20	166	100 beds available for Government cases.
Guy's - - -	20	17	Number reduced from 24 and 30 respectively.
Middlesex - -	12	8	
St. Bartholomew's -	26	24	One additional male bed, but female beds reduced lately from 50 to 24.
St. Thomas' - -		30	Males admitted into Surgical Wards.

G

Appendix. No. 3.

Return showing the accommodation appropriated to Venereal Inpatients at the various Hospitals and Infirmaries in the following towns and cities.

Town or City.	Hospital or Infirmary.	Beds. Males.	Beds. Females.	Remarks.
Aberdeen	Royal Infirmary	5	8	
Belfast	Royal Hospital	—		Males admitted free, females only on payment. No special beds.
	Charitable Infirmary	None.	None.	
Birmingham	General Hospital			Cases admitted, but no special beds.
	Queen's Hospital	8	7	In detached wards.
Brighton	Sussex County Hospital	None.	None.	Only exceptional cases taken in.
Bristol	General Hospital	None.	None.	Only exceptional cases admitted.
	Royal Infirmary	None.	None.	
Cardiff	Cardiff, Glamorganshire and Monmouthshire Infirmary	None.	None.	Rules exclude such cases.
	Adelaide Hospital			Cases admitted. Beds not limited.
	City of Dublin Hospital			Cases admitted. No special beds.
	Dr. Steven's Hospital	15	None.	Females only exceptionally admitted.
	Jervis St. Hospital			Only exceptional cases.
Dublin	Mater Misericordiæ Hospital			Only urgent cases admitted. No special beds.
	Meath Hospital	None.	None.	Excluded by Act of Parliament.
	Mercer's Hospital			Urgent cases admitted. No special beds.
	Richmond Hospital			Cases admitted. No limited number of beds.

APPENDIX No. 3.— *Continued.*

Town or City.	Hospital or Infirmary.	Beds.		Remarks.
		Males.	Females.	
Dublin—*Continued*	Sir Patrick Dun's -			Cases, both male and female, admitted into Surgical wards.
	St. Vincent's -			Only cases of secondary diseases admitted.
Edinburgh - -	Royal Infirmary -		16	Males admitted into general wards.
Glasgow - -	Royal Infirmary -	12	None.	
Hull - - -	General Infirmary -			No special beds. Patients admitted and isolated as much as possible.
Leeds - - -	General Infirmary -	None.	None.	Rules exclude all cases of venereal disease.
Liverpool - -	Northern Hospital -			Cases of tertiary syphilis occasionally admitted.
	Royal Infirmary -	None.	None.	Lock Hospital attached.
	Royal Southern Hospital - - -	.		A few males admitted on payment.
	Stanley Hospital -	None.	None.	Cases seen as out-patients.
Manchester - -	Salford and Pendleton Royal Hospital	None.	None.	Rules exclude such cases.
	Royal Infirmary -			No special beds, but cases admitted.
Newcastle-on-Tyne	The Infirmary - -	14	12	Females admitted free, males only on payment.
Sheffield - -	General Infirmary -			Cases not admitted; rules exclude.
	Public Hospital -	None.	None.	Cases admitted. special beds.
Wolverhampton -	Wolverhampton and Staffordshire General Hospital -			Only exceptional cases admitted. No special beds.

www.ingramcontent.com/pod-product-compliance
Lightning Source LLC
Chambersburg PA
CBHW021417090426
42742CB00009B/1174